IF YOU *really* LOVED me...

IF YOU *really* LOVED me...

TOBY GREEN

RANDOM HOUSE
AUSTRALIA

Random House Australia Pty Ltd
20 Alfred Street, Milsons Point, NSW 2061

Sydney New York Toronto
London Auckland Johannesburg
and agencies throughout the world

First published in 1996

National Library of Australia
Cataloguing-in-Publication Data

Green, Toby.
If you *really* loved me: the no-nonsense how-to-get-a-life guide to relationships.

Includes index.
ISBN 0 09 183260 8.

I. Interpersonal relations. 2. Man-woman relationships.
I. Title.

158.2

Design by Yolande Gray
Typeset by Midland Typesetters, Maryborough
Printed by Griffin Paperbacks, Adelaide

Contents

Dedication   viii

Acknowledgments   x

Introduction   xi

Getting to Know Yourself   1

Filet mignon or meat pie?   3

Personal best   9

How to deflect a guilt trip   13

Owning your own choices   18

Returning to the scene of the crime   23

Surviving a Relationship — Making it Work   29

If you're hot, you're hot   31

I'm here aren't I? … dealing with the 'C' word   37

Getting men wrong   40

Getting men right   46

How to negotiate and win   52

How are you, how are you *really*?   57

That couldn't happen to me   62

Sharks in the water   66

I'll have what they're having   71

Oh no! I've done it again   78

Tossing out the old   84
Please paddle my canoe   89
Learning to paddle together   96

Sex and Sensuality   101
Sleeping with friends   103
Kiss and tell   108
Is there life after infidelity?   112
It was just sex   119
Are you a good lover?   125
Getting women right   131

All in the Family   135
Mum and Dad, meet Kylie   137
'My little man' and 'Daddy's little princess'   142
Teenagers — a therapist's nightmare   149
The unkindest cut of all   156
Disenfranchised grandparents   162
The Brady Bunch nightmare   166

Time for Change   173
Leopards can change their spots   175
No-win special   180
Chequebook tyranny   186
Winning versus being right   193
Rebound relationships   199

Getting Help — Before, During and After   205

'I do' … I think   207

Friends and mates   213

Curing a broken heart   217

Creative divorce   221

Shrink shopping   227

Tobyisms   235

Suggested Reading   237

Index   238

Dedication

My father was reputed to be one of the best surgeons on the north shore of Boston. He was one of those old-fashioned types who made house calls in the middle of the night and was never out of phone reach to patients. After twenty-five years of being a successful surgeon, Dad was still happy to barter an appendectomy for cabbage rolls, lasagna and matzah balls.

He only ever drove Chevrolets because he thought it obscene to be ostentatious with money earned through people's suffering.

When asked what he did for a living his answer was, 'I deal in precious cargo.' That's what he believed.

In the summer of 1963, he grabbed an anti-Vietnam placard out of my hand, insisted I put on a hint of lipstick, not to mention shoes, and show up the next morning at his medical clinic.

I was to sit at the front desk, answer phones, take accurate messages and in general be an asset to the patients in the waiting room. Under absolutely no circumstances was I to discuss politics with anyone.

This is my favourite story from that summer. Sal DeLisio

was the rubbish contractor for the clinic. First-generation Italian–American, he had started out as a council garbage man and ended up with a fleet of trucks and a contracting empire. Sal attended to Dad's clinic personally. One Friday, rubbish removal day, Dad instructed me to bring two cups of coffee for Sal and himself to number 1 surgery and hold all calls between 9.00 and 9.30 a.m.

I had never known Dad to be out of telephone reach, ever. Four Fridays later, I realised Sal wasn't sick. This was a ritual. I plucked up the courage and asked, 'Dad, I don't get it. What on earth do you and Sal talk about every Friday morning?'

He said, 'Toby, you may not understand this, but you can get to a point in life when you are so busy, so absorbed in what you're doing, that you can actually lose touch with what's going on in the real world. On Fridays, Sal teaches me about life.'

There is a God.
I know.
I spent time with him.

This book is dedicated to
Dr Louis Edward Barron (1906–1965)

Acknowledgments

I would like to thank my clientele for teaching me everything I know; for their bravery in addressing hard issues; for their willingness to expose their most vulnerable inner beings; and for their trust in allowing me to be the midwife at the birth of their real selves.

Thanks must go to the following: Tim Clucas for putting me out there in spite of my accent; Clare Murphy for discovering something in me I had no idea existed; my mother, who has perpetually been my matron of honour in life and who could teach Norman Vincent Peale a thing or two; my sons Christopher and Jeremy, who have caused me to discover scary, previously unexplored sections of my heart that no-one else has touched; and my husband Ross, the living embodiment of commitment who has truly been 'the wind beneath my wings'.

Introduction

The halcyon days of therapists being able to cross their arms behind their heads, settle into their leather lounges and fill an hour with the three textbook shrink utterances: 'Uh-huh,' 'How long have you been feeling this way?' and 'What makes you think that?' are over.

Clients are demanding quick, comprehensive answers to their problems; not hypothesis and theory. In my practice, I have had to cultivate a much more accessible shorthand methodology for getting people where they want to go, faster, with more feedback, focus and clarity.

My technique is one of short, sharp shots — sweetened with a touch of humour to help the medicine go down. I ascribe the level of success I have achieved over eighteen years of practice to this style. It is in this spirit that I have set out to translate into written word the same effective application.

The media talks about getting information across in grabs. Food is takeaway. Dishes and nappies are disposable. Computers and refrigerators have built-in obsolescence. Supermarket goods have use-by dates. Tempers are short, and so is attention. Relationships are also short. Is it any wonder people have come to think commitment means 'I'm here as long as I'm having fun, the sex is great and the living is easy'?

It is my belief, and my experience within my practice, that if there were answers that could be made simple and clear enough, people would gladly grasp them to their consciousness and derive all the elusive joy that successful relationships hold. *If You* really *Loved Me* ... has been written to answer this need. It's time to have on offer a self-help book that is as enjoyable to read as spy stories and murder mysteries, while at the same time perfecting relationships.

In this book you'll find every relationship issue you'll ever encounter, from fear of abandonment to overzealousness! No matter what the problem, in three- or four-page chapters, you'll have the solution at your fingertips. The problems are all based on real-life cases, so here's an opportunity to peep through the keyhole and discover what problems others are wrestling with. If you already have a great relationship, give the book to those who don't, or just enjoy the read, smug in the knowledge that you would never make the same mistakes ...

If You really *Loved Me* ... will take you on a journey through relationships. Just what is a relationship, this something we enter into with someone else? It suggests words like liaison, partnership, alliance. It is important to get ourselves fit and ready for the task ahead. If we want to move towards really understanding another, then we must begin by having an understanding of who we are ourselves. Moving from the individual to a partnership, how do we form a link with this other? There are some issues that are so universal to all relationships that it's a good idea to be aware of them and armed with the skills to tackle them appropriately. These issues include jealousy, guilt, monogamy, sexuality, commitment, intimacy, not to mention family problems, just to name a few.

This book provides road maps to help you on the relationship journey and contingency plans for when you get stuck and need help. When the relationship just doesn't work and it's time for change, there are people who can help. Mostly, though, the book concentrates on reaching the destination of workable, successful, alive, empowered and joyous partnerships with others and happiness within ourselves.

As an avowed men's libber, with a predominantly male practice, I think you'll find this book offers a welcome change to the male ego-bashing that most of us are getting pretty bored with. If you're male, you'll find this book user-friendly. If you're female, you may learn to get your sense of humour back about the men in your life or discover a way to more easily communicate with them.

If 'no pain, no gain' has become tedious, you're ready for *If You* really *Loved Me* ... It is long past the time to lighten up. If you believe that laughter is the best answer for pain, when was the last time a self-help book made you laugh? It's time one did.

Getting to KNOW yourself

One of the reasons relationships are stretched to breaking point is that they are mostly entered into in the spirit of solution seeking. In other words, if my life doesn't go all that well with me driving it, perhaps the answer is to get myself another driver. Maybe with them at the steering wheel, things will go better: 'Here, over to you.' Nice try, but it won't work.

One-half times one-half equals one-quarter. It's true in mathematics and it's true in relationships. Only one whole plus one whole equals two. Relationships fail because people are coming from scarcity, not from abundance. A relationship has to be about what each person has to contribute to it, not what they can get out of it. 'I need you' is heavy. 'I don't need you, but I choose you' is liberating to both parties.

The first step in relationship contemplation is doing some homework. If you can't stand your own company, what makes you think it's all right to inflict yourself on someone else? Why do you act in certain ways? Who exactly are you? What is there about you that you don't like or can't accept? How well do you get on with other people? Partners, get to know thy selves.

Filet Mignon
or
Meat Pie?

Professionally speaking, the three little words that send shivers down my spine are 'Who am I?' Honestly, that one really stumps me. I have a friend who asked me, 'Am I as fat as that lady?' It had the same impact. How can someone not know what they look like? How can someone not know who they are? Some people just don't.

The reason the question is daunting is that it's hard to figure out where to start. If a person has no sense of 'I', then to whom am I having the pleasure of speaking? So to speak.

The following is a true story. My son asked if I would be willing to take a friend of his with us on a holiday. I hadn't seen Mike for a while, but I felt close to him and he considered me an aunty. I said yes. When he joined us, I was horrified. Mike had turned into a right proper jerk. He was your typical late-adolescent Mr Hip and Groovy. All jargon and pose. I actually found it hard to be in the same room with him.

I did what I always do in circumstances where someone's

behaviour makes me not know how to be around them. I removed myself from being in a relationship with him. I didn't ignore him, but I turned down my energy level for relating to match his. Mike wasn't interested in relating, only in impressing. He was only concerned with his performance, with which he obviously was pleased. It also worked for my son, who was impressed. He never even noticed my lack of audience participation.

We were going to be together for two weeks. One rule was that all phone calls had to be placed after 5.00 p.m. when rates went down. It got so bad listening to Mike being groovy on the phone that I had to keep moving my chair down the veranda in order to read, out of earshot.

A week into our stay, Mike came down the veranda and asked, 'What do you think of me?' This is a common response people have to being put in psychological purgatory. It has a subliminal effect that eventually gives the other person a sense of being disconnected. (Unless they are frontal lobotomy material. Mike wasn't that bad.)

I answered, 'You're not going to like my answer, so I'm inviting you to take back your question.'

'What do you mean?'

'Mike, I mean that you are not going to be pleased with what I'm going to say, so I think it's only fair I tell you that, so you can take back the question.'

'What could it be?'

'Mike, sit down. I think you're being a jerk. I think what comes out of your mouth is rubbish. I think it's all an act. And I have absolutely no idea who the real Mike is.'

'But I think the "me" I'm being *is* the real me. If this isn't me, then who am I?'

It was out of this encounter that I devised the 'two voices' theory. My observation is that people have two separate voices they listen to. First is the voice of 'should do, should be'. If you were to stick your fingers in your ears, this voice would be located somewhere in the middle of your head, saying: 'I should do this. They should do that. I should say this. They shouldn't act that way.' It's the voice of judgment, point of view and opinion.

The second is the voice of 'the truth for you'. If you place one finger on your chest bone and another on your belly button, it's somewhere in the middle and about five centimetres in. It's the gut or heart voice. This voice says what you really want. When the waiter says 'Tonight's specials are filet mignon or meat pie,' you might order filet mignon to impress a date but it's the meat pie you really want.

The predicament with the two voices is that the voice of 'should do, should be' is very loud, because it's a proving, impressing, in-need-of-agreement voice. The voice of 'the truth for you' is quiet. The truth just is. It doesn't have to prove anything. Your real self lies in the voice of the truth for you. In order to find your real self you need to get the voice of 'should do, should be' to shut up. But first you need to know the difference between the two.

What I advised Mike to do was to start listening to which voice he was tuned into. I told him to check in often to see if he really meant what he was saying, to ask himself, 'Is this really the truth for me?'

The two weeks were up. We all went back to our respective homes. I asked Mike to keep in touch. I wanted to know how he was proceeding.

First phone call: 'Toby, I think I'm schizophrenic.'

'What happened?'

'You know my friend, Robert? Well, my flatmate, John, caught Robert using his new Walkman. John told Robert off in such a cool way that I decided that if Robert used my Walkman, I'd say the same thing to him as John did. Then this really weird thing happened. From somewhere inside me came this voice asking, "How do you really feel about Robert using your Walkman?" Of course I couldn't care less, so why was I going to give a speech about something I don't even care about?'

'Congratulations, Mike, you've just experienced the two voices. The cool speech-giver was the voice of "should do, should be". I should be hip and groovy like John. And the second voice was the voice of "the truth for you", which is that you really wouldn't mind Robert using your Walkman. Now that you've done it once, at least you know the two voices exist and you can differentiate between them. No, far from being schizophrenic, you've just discovered the voice of your real self.'

The following is a gender generalisation. Men often identify themselves by facts and thoughts. Feasibility study would be right up a male alley: 'I think, therefore I am.' Thinking is one aspect of knowing your real self, it is only a part of what defines us.

A man decides to buy a new car. After months of deliberation and studying reports on durability, maintenance and best value for money, he's convinced that a Volvo is the car for him.

So he buys one and can't understand why he feels miserable about it. The reason is that in his travels through car-yards he spied a second-hand 1950 MGB, which he fell in love with. He never 'thought' about it as a possibility because, in more ways than he could count, there was no way it could have passed his feasibility study. In *fact* it made no sense. Although the Volvo added up on paper, the truth for him was the MGB. By not being true to himself, he bought the wrong car.

Women tend to define themselves as, 'I feel, therefore I am.' This is not the whole picture either. If you were to take the above scenario and insert a woman, it would be likely that because of her emotional response to the MGB, she would have chosen it. Unless she has automotive know-how or a lifestyle that supports her having an older, high-maintenance car, she's made an impractical choice. The Volvo may have been smarter. 'Although I feel far more emotionally attracted to the MGB, the truth for me is that I'd feel more secure with the Volvo.'

'I think', therefore 'I should', and 'I feel', therefore 'I should' still come under the voice of 'should do, should be'. The real you has to take both thoughts *and* feelings into consideration. Having done that, the answer should reside in the voice of 'the truth for you', which may not be the result of either thoughts or feelings. You'll feel the liberation of being able to say, 'I know this makes absolutely no sense, in terms of how I feel or what is logical, but what I'm going to do, say, choose is ...'

Now you can see why I say that the most important thing is to be able to listen and differentiate between the two voices. When you do, the authentic 'I am' — your real self — will become clear and feel more natural. You will then begin to see your job, goals and possessions as an extension of, not a substitute for, your real self. If they disappear, you don't.

For example: I am Toby Green. I am a psychologist. I am married to Ross Green. I am the mother of Christopher and Jeremy. I drive a Honda. If everything else disappears, the only thing that remains is that I am still Toby Green. You will learn that everything that comes after your name is simply the individual and unique manifestation of what is your own special, distinctive, one-of-a-kind *self*-expression.

Once we become clearer about who we are, we can define our goals more clearly.

Personal Best

My husband and I were sitting at a cafe. A young man sat down next to us. On the back of his T-shirt was the logo 'Second place is the first loser'. I felt myself getting angry.

I thought about Craig. Craig's marriage wasn't working all that well. Craig is a list-maker, a goal-setter, a fiscal organiser, and a holiday, business and leisure planner. He is also a contract maker, so that those associated with him will stick by the plans. Craig is a perfectionist.

I give you fair warning. When someone tells you they are a perfectionist, duck. The hidden agenda with perfectionism is that only one person on the planet ever gets it right — them. Everyone else does it half-baked. Perfectionism is a high-falutin term for being judgmental and intolerant.

In all fairness, perfectionists are as hard on themselves as they are on others, perhaps harder. It's no fun being a perfectionist. It's also no fun being married to one.

Craig and Marilyn had a prenuptial agreement about Marilyn's financial contribution to their partnership. It was a signed contract.

Marilyn is hopeless at finances. She grew up in a wealthy family and has no innate interest or knowledge concerning the value of money. Her motto is: If you have it, spend it, if you don't, don't. She signed the contract out of naivety. She thought, 'How hard could it be?' Hard enough to be the cause of a marriage melt down.

Marilyn was in charge of managing the household budget. She had to keep track of income and expenditure, and estimate how much money they'd need to spend each month. Sometimes she ended up with a balanced chequebook, sometimes she had money left over and at other times expenditures exceeded those budgeted for. She had no idea what contributed to what result and it drove Craig nuts.

Marilyn wanted to buy a car. Craig did an extensive feasibility study, discussing with Marilyn the costs involved, and asked if she was sure she could meet her expenses. She said she was pretty sure she could. She bought the car but she found she couldn't meet her expenses. She then said it was all right if Craig got rid of the car and she meant it. Craig earns a good salary. He could assume the repayments with ease. That wasn't the issue.

This kind of deadlock had happened before. Either Craig would bale out Marilyn and feel resentful or he'd refuse to help her and feel guilty like Scrooge. Craig accused her of sabotaging and baiting. Marilyn accused him of intolerance and conditional love. As for me, I was confused.

Was Marilyn deliberately setting Craig up as punishment for his expectations of her? Or was she really not able to come to terms with the responsibilities for which she had signed on?

In either case, the only way I could see Craig finding out the truth was for him to let go of Marilyn's outcome. If he could do that, he'd see whether Marilyn was a rebel or inept.

Easier said than done. Craig was terrified he'd find out he had a bimbo on his hands. Then what would he do? I asked him why he had been attracted to Marilyn in the first place. He said he found her exuberant, affectionate, fun to be with and she made him laugh. You'd have to be blind not to see that when she wasn't cowering to protect her self-esteem, she adored him.

Perfectionists are easily challenged. Craig went to work on himself. Because the rules were that he was not allowed to evaluate Marilyn, his judgment turned elsewhere. He found a well of sadness about his childhood. Craig recalled memories of being chubby, unathletic, left out and lonely. He'd felt inadequate growing up. Even as a successful, professional adult he always measured his success in comparison to his colleagues.

He also measured his success in comparison to his own projections. His house was the house he was having until he could afford his 'real' house. He didn't have his 'real' car yet, or holiday or income. What was becoming apparent was that because Marilyn didn't meet his expectations, she couldn't be his 'real' wife.

Craig enjoyed the non-competitive sports of surfing and long-distance running. What he really wanted to do was join a local running club, which had an annual race some 30 kilometres long. At first Craig refused to join until he had trained enough to be assured of a substantial placing in the race. Then he relented: he wasn't ready to be sure of achieving that goal but he joined anyway. The goal he now set for himself was to finish the race. Long after the better runners won, placed and finished, Craig dragged himself, exhausted, across the line.

This was Craig's first experience of feeling that who he was, as he was, was enough. His own personal best was quite adequate for him. At last he had permission from himself simply to do his best. If that wasn't the best in the race, it still qualified for a mark on his personal scoreboard.

The natural flow-on from this self-approval was an easier ability to extend the same sense of permission to Marilyn. He saw that someone without her exuberance, love of fun and ability to laugh might not have been able to put up with his judgmental, rigid, perfectionist self.

With the pressure of Craig's expectations taken away, Marilyn's capacity for managing her money is measurably better. Will she be able to sustain these results? Time will tell. She may never be written up in *Fortune* magazine's top 100, but in the meantime she's no longer the wife he's putting up with until she passes muster to qualify as his 'real' wife. Who she is, as she is, is good enough for Craig to be happily committed.

Second place is the first loser? To whom?

When you learn greater self-acceptance it becomes easier to accept others.

At the same time, as we'll see, it's also important to set limits and establish personal boundaries.

How to Deflect
a Guilt Trip

It was Tuesday evening. Lynn picked up the phone. Her fingers were shaking. She dialled the number.

Lynn: 'Mum? Hi. It's me. Look, I was just wondering … the girls in the office are planning a farewell party for the receptionist who's getting married and I wonder if you'd mind terribly if I didn't come for dinner tomorrow night?'

Mum: 'It must be nice spending time around people who are happily making plans for the future. I wish I was lucky enough to be enjoying someone's companionship. Then I wouldn't have to depend on looking forward all week to Wednesday night — the only night of the week I can count on having some company. That is, unless my daughter doesn't get a better offer. But that seems to be happening more and more often.'

Lynn: 'The last time I missed a Wednesday was when I was in bed with the flu.'

Mum: 'You should have watched "Oprah" today. They were talking about psychosomatic disease, and how powerful the mind is when we want to get out of things.'

Lynn: 'Never mind, Mum. I'll be there for dinner.'

Mum: 'Don't worry about me. I'll be fine on my own. God knows I'm used to it.'

Lynn: 'I'll see you at 7.00.'

Haven't we all had a mother, boss, neighbour or in-law who knew exactly where to insert the knife and just how much to twist it to get us to jump through whatever hoop they had in mind?

Guilt. Nice person's disease. Guilt is an emotion we feel when we do something we think is bad. If we feel bad about what we've done, that lets us know we're really a nice person. Everyone knows only terrible people do bad things and don't feel bad.

What a waste of time! If you're going to do something bad, identify it as 'I'm going to do something bad'. Weigh it up. If it's worth doing, take responsibility for it, then do it and call it what it is. If it's not worth doing because of how you're going to feel afterwards, don't do it.

Easily said. Unfortunately, most of us are given an overdose of what Freud called 'superego', or our self-critical, parental identity. We're socialised into believing that what people think of us is more important than learning to state the truth in a polite, depersonalised manner. As a result, we're slaves to others' opinions of us, instead of being honest and getting our needs met.

From where I'm sitting, society looks like it got divided into the 'users' and the 'used'. The users figured out this 'nice person' phenomenon a long time ago. It works perfectly for them. They have radar ability to hone in on the used. They know they can employ them to their advantage any time they like. The users make sure they get their needs met.

The used, or 'nice people', are the user's easy mark, but the system works just as well for them. Approval is the used person's principal motivation. The used need people for whom they can perform good deeds. The reward for these deeds is approval. Since they have a self-concept of being nice, the user's endorsement reaffirms that they are right about their self-image. Self-righteousness is, after all, about being 'self-right'. In this way, the used are getting their needs met as well.

The one thing you have to be careful about around a used person is the resentment factor. Resentment is where you ask me to do something for you and I really don't want to do it. But I don't let you know that. If I do, you may think I'm not nice. So I do what you ask, but I'm secretly angry at you for asking me. If you sense this you may ask me, 'What's wrong?' I'll answer, 'Nothing' or, 'Don't worry about it' or 'If you don't know what's wrong, never mind.'

If you're one of the used and want out, there is a price to pay. There are people who are going to think you are not nice, especially users who have become dependent upon you. So, if you're not ready to cash in your self-image, wait until you are.

Here's an example of a false start. A client asked me if anyone ever told me that my therapy turned people into cold, heartless beings. I asked her what she meant. She had been in a card group for many years, with a group of women who lived in the same suburb. One of the women got divorced and received the settlement from Hell. She went from a large home in an expensive neighbourhood to a one-bedroom unit,

45 minutes away and no car. My client felt so sorry for her that she insisted on driving the 180 minutes it took to pick up and deliver this woman to and from their card group.

Then, as a result of therapy, my client announced that she didn't want to do the driving any more. She offered to instead split taxi costs with the divorced woman. This woman told my client that she was the last person she thought would 'let her down'. My client had a hard time grappling with the idea of being seen as 'that kind of person'. Her option was a three-hour delivery service or an unkind self-image. She tried both and decided to opt for being unpopular.

If you're ready to switch from being nice to being true to your needs, here are some tips.

When someone asks something from you, look at it pretty hard. Can you do it gladly and stay true to yourself? Are you being honest? Is their opinion of you or getting your needs met more important? Are you willing to be disapproved of?

If the request being made of you doesn't suit, you can use the 'good news, bad news' technique. 'I really love you, Mum, but I'm not coming for dinner on Wednesday.' 'I think you're a terrific guy, but I don't think there's any point in our going out with each other any more.' 'I love having you at card nights, I'm just too exhausted to drive three hours to transport you.' 'I think you're a wonderful boss, Terry. Please get your hand off my knee.'

Delivering the good news disallows the 'If you really loved, liked, cared ...' accusations. It assists the user in not taking your knock-back personally. Delivering the bad news allows you to be honest, to be true to yourself. It permits you to get your needs met and stops you from being resentful. You will find yourself liking the user more, because you can trust yourself to set limits around them.

If the user is a master at using others, they will have a plethora of their own techniques. The main thrust of them will be aimed at making you feel bad about yourself. Many of them start with or imply 'What kind of a person would ... ?'

Here are some replies intended to deflect a guilt trip:

'That must be terrible for you.'

'I'd hate it if I saw things that way.'

'I'd be depressed if I had those problems, too.'

'I'd detest it if that were happening to me.'

'No wonder you look so worried and unhappy. I would be if I were in your shoes.'

These deflections let the user know that you empathise with their complaint, but aren't going to be manipulated into fixing the problem. Even the best users know when they're beaten. Be consistent. Stand your ground.

If you're good at being a user, don't worry. There will always be an endless supply of 'nice folk' who thrive on doing good deeds and self-righteousness. They'll be grateful for the trade-off of your approval.

When you act true to your own needs, your new-found self-esteem and attitude will help you decide what *you* want to do, without being influenced or manipulated by others. You're now on the road to owning your own choices.

Owning Your Own Choices

Kerry: 'Richard suffers from terminal stubbornness. There's only one month to go and I want out before then. I've had it.'

Richard: 'This is the stupidest thing I've ever heard of. Have you ever heard of a case where a marriage ended over a Valentine's Day card?'

Kerry: 'Forget it. It doesn't matter any more. It will never be a problem for you again.'

Richard: 'I keep telling her if she'd stop nagging, she'd get what she wants.'

Kerry: 'If I don't nag, you don't listen. Half the time I don't know if you've heard me or not. Or if you have heard me, whether you'll do as I've suggested or not. You always say "yeah, yeah, yeah" whether you are intending to do as I ask or not.'

Richard's eyes do a 'give me a break' roll.

'OK. What's going on here?' I ask.

'I feel like I'm in a no-win special,' Kerry complains. 'It doesn't matter what I ask, he won't do it. It's as though just because I have asked, it's the very thing he won't do. My punishment for wanting something is that's what I won't get.'

'Tell me about the Valentine's Day card,' I suggest.

'Well, call me sentimental,' Kerry says, 'but I've told Richard there are only two celebrations that matter to me: one is my birthday and the other is Valentine's Day. I don't want big expensive gifts. I would just like Richard to take out a few minutes twice a year. I'd like him to give me a little consideration and buy a card that shows he's thought about me.'

'Richard, what's the problem?'

'I don't know how to explain it exactly. I just feel like I can't do what she wants because she's spoiled it by asking for it. It's like, now I'm expected to do it, so it takes all the surprise out of it.'

When I was taking down Richard's biography, he started to talk about his mother. 'She was dominating, overbearing and obsessed with what other people thought. Everything was done for the sake of appearances. I really wanted to please her. I kept trying to win her approval but nothing I ever did was good enough. She could make me feel really bad about myself.

'My school results weren't all that great and she said I'd do better if I went to a private school. When I went to the private school, I worked really hard and got top grades. I overheard her telling a friend on the phone how well I'd done. She was saying that if it hadn't been for her, "God knows what would have become of him." She would never tell me to my face how well I'd done. On top of that, she didn't give me credit for how hard I worked. She made out that the reason I succeeded was her insistence on a private school.

'I felt like I was some kind of trophy she marched out to impress people with when it suited her. That was the last time I ever tried to please her. I flunked out after that, to her great shame and horror. What would she tell her friends? I vowed I would never be dominated by anyone ever again.'

'Richard, do you have anything against Valentine cards per se?'

'Yes. I see them as a manipulation. I think Valentine's Day is an excuse for the card companies to make people feel bad about not buying a card for someone. I think they commercialised Valentine's Day because there were no reasons to buy cards between New Year and Easter. I feel like if I buy one, they're saying to themselves, "Got you in, sucker!"'

'Do you have anything against buying presents per se?'

'No. I'm a generous person. I think Kerry would agree that I'm not tight with money.'

Kerry nods affirmatively.

Richard's predicament has narrowed itself down to a very common problem. Some people feel dominated or manipulated by meeting another's expectations. They feel as though if they do the requested or expected thing, they are being dominated by the person and the request they are meeting. The only way these people can maintain their independence is to deny the request and not meet the expectation.

Such people can appear stubborn, rebellious and selfish, but it's not always that simple. Often they feel uncomfortable because they are caught in a no-win situation. They would like to please their partner, but they can't without losing their autonomy. When their partner gets upset, they are unhappy and frustrated. But they can see no solution. They feel suffocated and controlled.

When asked whether this is a fair description of Richard's dilemma, he says 'yes'. When I point out that his behaviour is, in fact, totally predictable, controllable and easily manipulated, he is surprised. I explain that if he were my partner, I'd use reverse psychology. If I wanted him to move to the right, I'd tell him to move to the left. In that way he'd be forced every time to move to the right, exactly where I want him.

In order to get out of the bind, this is what Richard needs to do. If Kerry wants something, he needs to think about it. If he agrees that it's a reasonable suggestion, one that he would like to fulfil, he needs to see it independently. He needs to ask himself what he would do if he had thought of it himself.

If it's something he would do, he needs to see that he's free to do it for one reason only. He's doing it because that's what he wants to do, even if, *coincidentally*, someone else has suggested the same thing. He's not doing it because he's a helpless slave to her whims, he has free choice. He may choose to do it because it would make her happy, but, first of all, he's doing it for himself.

The penny drops. He can see his way clear to meeting Kerry's needs without feeling exploited, dominated and manipulated. She can be happy and he can remain his own person.

'Richard, picture the scene. You've given Kerry a Valentine's Day card. You walk into the house. You pick up the phone and unexpectedly hear Kerry on the line. She's talking to a representative from a card company who says he's doing a survey. The marketing department is trying to ascertain whether their advertising campaign has been effective. Does she have a man in her life and did he give her a card on Valentine's Day?

'Kerry is answering the man. She's saying, "Yes. Between your ad campaign and my nagging, at last we sucked him into buying me a card." Richard, how would you feel?'

'Kerry and the card man can think anything they want. I would know that I bought the card because that's what I decided I wanted to do. I bought it for one reason only. Because I chose to.'

When you start to own your own choices, you're beginning to drive your own bus rather than being driven by it. You understand that real freedom of choice allows you to choose to do something even though someone else might want you to do the same thing. But there are other issues that need to be dealt with before you get your hands on the wheel!

Returning
to the Scene
of the Crime

Her name is Caroline. 'I pick the most disastrous relation-ships. The thing they have in common is that the men I choose are all like my father. Why do I do that?' Fathers and daughters. Shakespeare wrote *King Lear* about them. Freud named a complex after them.

His name is Lex. 'This is the third relationship to fall down around me. All the women I date remind me of my mother.' Mothers and sons. They are important relationships. Sophocles wrote *Oedipus Rex* about them. Parents are the first people of the opposite sex who matter. How we get along with them sets the tone for how we'll get on with the opposite sex in the future. If all goes well, we'll settle for nothing less in our adult relationships. If it's been rocky, it's a different scenario.

When we don't have a good relationship with a parent, we end up standing on one foot, emotionally off-balance. We're left trying to find out how to get it right — how to get the approval, love, respect and the conflict-free relationship we didn't get with them. We're left feeling frustrated about how it went wrong. If we can score a 'win' with a symbolically similar person to our parent, we feel like we now know how we could have won with them and got it right.

So, the bizarre quest begins. The search is on for someone who disapproves of us the same way Dad did, or manipulates us like Mum did, or presents the same kind of conflict. We fantasise that when we're able to get this rejecting or difficult partner to love us, the way we wanted to be loved by our parents, then the imbalance will be remedied.

When we win with this partner, we feel that we've resolved what was unresolvable. The drive is to get this person to, finally, understand what is wonderful about us. If only our father or mother had experienced this, they would have realised how blessed they were to have us for a son or daughter. Then they would have loved us unconditionally.

If Dad or Mum was abusive, we need an abusive partner; if they were critical, we look for a critical partner. If they had high expectations of us, we look for someone who has high expectations. If they were manipulative, we need someone who is a manipulator. Then we tap dance as fast as we can, to get their approval. When we finally do, the dream is that we will, at last, have both feet on the ground — emotional balance.

The other reason we pick people who are like our parents involves a control issue. Let's say, like Caroline, we had a bad experience with our father; he was overly critical and humiliated us. Don't forget, when that humiliation started we were very young. When we're young, we're physically small and impotent. We're not very worldly wise, because we haven't had much experience to draw on. Therefore, we haven't got much control.

In other words, we can't make what's happening in our

environment stop. We don't have enough power to make an adult behave the way we need him or her to behave. Our well-being is in the hands of a person who may be quite inadequate for a position of responsibility. And we're stuck not being able to do anything about it. Depending on how menacing the circumstances are, it could feel like we won't survive emotionally and, in the extreme, physically.

In these cases, our *powerlessness* is actually worse than the bad behaviour. The daughter of a critical, humiliating father may say, 'When I grow up I'm never going to be with a man who is critical and humiliating.' What she thinks she's referring to are the feelings of degradation. She thinks her decision is about the bad feelings of being put down. It's not. This explains why so many daughters of abusive fathers end up with abusive husbands or boyfriends.

Her decision is about *impotency*. What she's really saying is, 'When I grow up, I'm never going to be with a man who is critical and humiliating, *out of my control.'* In other words, I had no control over the father I had, but if I pick a critical partner, then at least I've chosen him. I've walked into the relationship with my eyes wide open. There won't be any surprises. I'm in control because I selected him.

It goes like this. 'I expected my father to love me unconditionally and no matter how hard I tried, he'd criticise me. The disappointment and the feelings of being let down were too terrible to bear. If I have a partner who, subconsciously, I never expect to love me unconditionally, I'll never be surprised again. I may feel hurt and degraded, but not shocked, not impotent, and never out of control.'

Let's say, like Lex, we had a manipulative mother. She tried her darnedest to get us to do her bidding, her way, no matter how we felt about it. If we protested, she used emotional blackmail to make us feel so bad about our 'selfishness' or ingratitude for what she had sacrificed for us, that we began to feel she was usurping our power as a person. We felt that by fulfilling her needs, our own would never count.

What I say to myself is that when I grow up I will find a female who will never 'need' me the way my mother needed me. I want someone who will be strong enough to be able to look after her own emotional needs. She won't usurp my power by manipulating me into feeling bad if I don't behave the way she wants me to. I must never be out of control with a woman and let her emotionally dominate me.

Strangely enough, like Lex, we may pick emotional cripples who are always leaning on us to meet their needs. Or we choose healthy women, but every time they try to get a message across about a need or expectation, which everyone in a relationship will have, we'll hear them as 'getting at' us, even if that is not their intention. As the woman's frustration mounts, so will our perception of her as manipulative. This will eventually classify her as a control-grabbing, power-seeking, manipulative female, just like mother. But then we know all women are like that anyway!!

When worry about being hit by the bus of life becomes too much, sometimes it feels easier to throw ourselves under the bus. It's a way of being in control of our fate. We may be flattened, but we no longer have to live with the anxiety of worrying about when the bus is going to hit!

OK, so there we are, with as destructive a relationship in our adult life, as we had with dear old Dad or Mum. What do we do? The first thing is to realise that our mistake is in taking our parents personally. 'Very easy for you!' I hear you say. They certainly were looking at me when they were calling me 'stupid', 'clumsy', 'useless', 'selfish' and so on.

You probably weren't the only person your parent spoke to that way. That, most likely, was their style. I'm not saying it was fun or right, I'm saying it was just part of the way they were, as human beings. People who manipulate or have short fuses usually aren't selective. It's their nature. They can't help themselves. Commonly, they're poor communicators. They're usually critical out of frustration with themselves for not being able to better articulate what they want. They're bad at communicating their needs, so they use exploitation to take it out on others.

The other thing about our parents is that somehow, despite the way they loved (which may not have been great), we know that they did love us. We're just angry at the way they did it. And because they didn't love us the way we wanted them to, we're calling it 'not love'.

Imagine loving someone and expressing that love to them in French, because that's the only language you speak — and they say they won't consider it love, unless you say it in their language, which is Chinese! No matter how hard you try, you can't get it exactly right. We'd hate it if someone we loved did that to us.

We think it's cruel when someone doesn't say 'I love you' to someone they love. What's crueller still is to know, deep down, that someone does love us and pretends they don't.

It's father's and mother's day. There is something that can be done to stop the merry-go-round of destructive associations caused by bad dad/mum relationships. We need to resolve our relationships with them by letting them off the hook. I advise this more for us than for them.

If the partner in your life is really bad news, then you can get rid of them and all the bad news partners you've needed in order to act out the melodrama of your bad parent relationship. You won't need to find resolution with someone who isn't good for you, because you will have resolved things with your parents.

You won't need a destructive relationship for control purposes either. Through resolving your relationship with your parents, what you'll see is that no matter how bad they were, you did survive. As an adult, you no longer need control to be an issue that runs your life. Now you can concentrate on getting good news partners into your life, and on getting your needs met properly.

This can only be done if you're ready to cash in and be done with your victim scars. Those scars manifest the evidence of what your parent's behaviour has done to your life. They never meant you to take them personally. No-one would be more pleased to have your life turn out well than they would. We hated being judged, so do they. Go on. Give them a call. Let them know what you know; that in spite of their shortcomings, inadequacies and failings, they did love you. They just did it their way.

SURVIVING a Relationship- Making it Work

Before we even contemplate a relationship it's a good idea to understand what a relationship is. We have all been given a pretty distorted view, governed by Mills & Boon romances, country and western music and Hollywood schmaltz. It's time to get real. With a working definition—love, sexual chemistry and commitment—it is far more likely we'll be able to start off in a realistic direction.

OK, so now you're ready to get in there and give it a go. I think it only fair to warn you there are some relationship glitches that are so common they are almost clichés—communication deadlocks, denial of problems, jealousy, lack of commitment. Almost all of us will run into these issues at one time or another. It's better to be forewarned about what to do if one of them materialises. Remember, relationships are like journeys. There will be excitement and adventure, dull days and hairy times. Every situation that comes up will present you with a challenge. The way you handle each of them will determine how much you have learnt to stand up inside yourself — self-confident, worthy of respect and at peace with yourself.

In this section we also learn to come to terms with survival issues. These issues date back to something that happened to us when we were young, which felt awful and over which we had no control. It made us feel so terrible we wondered if we would survive, and we made a decision that we'd never let something like that happen to us again. This decision has meant that we can never again afford to be out of control. Until we make a new life decision and move on — even if this means a willingness to risk being devastated again — our relationships will suffer. You have to be in it to win it. Here are some survival techniques.

If You're Hot, You're Hot

An American psychologist named Abraham Maslow had a good idea. He noticed that for centuries, when looking for cures to the human condition, scientists classically studied sick people. The idea was that if a solution could be found for how to make people well, therein would lie the answers to why they got sick. Abe said, 'Why not study the anatomy of healthy people and see what makes them tick? Then we can use them as a model for how to stay healthy.' Not a bad idea.

In this book, I mostly talk about how to fix a relationship after it's damaged or broken. Taking Abe's advice, I thought it might be interesting to look at what makes for a good relationship.

Relationships that have lots of zing, seem to be compromise-free and have a certain *je ne sais quoi* always seem to contain three distinct characteristics: *love, chemistry* and *commitment.* One of them can't be fixed if it's not there, one is not so important and the other is imperative.

Chemistry can't be fixed. It is the physical part of a

relationship, the sexual component. It means magnetism, sensuality, being turned on, animal attraction. If chemistry exists it exists, and if it doesn't, forget it (except for an exception I'll cover later).

All of us, at some time, meet a new person and draw up a mental list of their good and bad points. In the left column are all the positives: polite, intelligent, ambitious, sense of humour, sensitive, perceptive, nice friends and OK parents. On the right side live the negatives. There's only one. Do I want to go to bed with him or her? No way!

Rip up the list and forget the relationship. If there's even minor arousal, for sure pursue it to see if any chemistry develops. If you've never had so much as a tingle of sexual stirring, no amount of justifying, rationalising or intelligent debate will make it happen. Don't waste each other's time. If you're hot, you're hot, if you're not, you're not.

Here is the exception. You did at some point have sexual feelings for this person but they've gone away. Hang in there to find out why. There's such a thing as diminished sexual feeling for a purpose. It can be a protection against intimacy. Let's say it's going along well sexually. Suddenly you realise your feelings are getting away from you. You're afraid of not being in control of your emotions. One good way of putting on the brakes is to withhold sexually. At least then there's an area where you feel in control, removed, distanced, safe.

The same sexual disappearing act can happen if there's fear of commitment. How many times have I heard that everything was fine sexually while courting. Then the relationship escalated into moving in with each other, engagement or marriage. All goes quiet on the southern front. By withholding sexually, you're in there, but not all the way. You can still back up, shut down, get out.

Commitment, for some people, feels like domination, like being overpowered by the partner to whom you're meant to commit. Withholding sex is a way of hanging onto power and retaining mastery of yourself. It keeps your partner from getting on top of you, so to speak.

Another sexual suppressant is loss of respect. Your partner does something you consider weak, such as being unable to make a decision or give a commitment, and you see that as feeble. You may see them as having unrealistic expectations of what your role is supposed to be — all-supportive, all-protective — which they use as an excuse for not taking responsibility for becoming a person in their own right.

Wedding night turn-off is not uncommon and may have nothing to do with performance. For a woman, it can have to do with her concept of the role of wife. If she takes her role model from her mother, whom she perceives as cold and sexless, she may feel this is the proper way to be. She's now moved from the carefree role of lover to what she sees as the respectable, responsible role of wife.

Conversely, the man may no longer see her as lover with the attendant romance, seduction, excitement. Now he may see her as wife, with wifely duties including conjugal rights. Over-night he switches in attitude from treating her specially to treating her as a wife object, no longer needing the lover's niceties. Nothing is a bigger wet blanket to sexuality than being taken for granted.

All of the above are fixable. They involve attitude changes and not basic sexual instinct changes. If you get the attitudes back in place with some constructive counselling or good communication, then the sexual feelings should come back as well. As long as sexual feelings were previously there, they should be redeemable.

Love. Love is the least important aspect of a relationship. Love is good for country and western music, teenagers and Mills & Boon addicts. We're coming at love in such a distorted way, and living in such alienated times, that we've actually come to see love as a rarity. If it shows up for even a second we grab it and try to hold onto it like a precious jewel, because it may not come again. This may be our only chance. This is a statement about the times we live in, not about love. Love is what should be there, everywhere, all the time, when anger and alienation and judgment are suspended.

When people ask, 'What is love?' I ask whether they have any children or pets, or have ever woken up on a perfect day, or been overwhelmed by a magic sunset. That feeling is love. Love is feeling part of the universe, a participant, a recipient, alive. Because we live our lives in such a pressured, competitive, estranged way, we have actually come to see love as the exception instead of the rule. The Beatles said it, 'All you need is love. Love is all you need.'

Adult, mature, romantic love comes and goes. It ebbs and flows within a relationship. There are times in marriage when you can feel overwhelmed by feelings of closeness to your partner. There are other times when you can feel numb, distant and angry. Then, during a distant spell, you might catch sight of your partner walking along the street and think your heart is going to burst through your shirt.

Most relationships go through a besotted phase, because when two people come together there is a new oneness, the excitement of discovery, the raw sexuality. It is a phase and a good launching pad for a relationship, but not a standard or a norm for a prolonged relationship. If it were, we'd all die of heart attacks before our first anniversaries, and have no time or energy for the real world.

When the exaggerated love settles back into everyday realistic relationship love, it should be the kind of love we have ordinarily for special things: a child, a pet, a perfect sunset.

In my opinion, love is cheap, as in inexpensive. Love is easy. On a good day I love my butcher. I love the postie. My partner is the person I love, and with whom I'm doing something about it. Which brings us to the third ingredient.

Commitment. Commitment is the most important aspect of relationship (as long as there's chemistry). Commitment is the spirit of a relationship. It's the spirit of 'only you', the spirit of 'forever'. Commitment is the glue, the cement that's there when nothing else is. When you feel like bopping your partner over the head with a frying pan, it's not love, lust or passion that gets you home, it's commitment.

Commitment is easy when everything is ideal. Why would anyone leave when everything is fun, sexy, laughter-filled? When relationships are shaky, which they all are at one time or another, it's the ability to commit that carries you through.

I mentioned 'only you', 'forever' and 'spirit'. The spirit determines the quality of the commitment. If a commitment is made in a spirit of meanness and sacrifice, it will feel different from a commitment made in the spirit of contribution, participation, loving patience and humour. If you've got the strength, determination and fortitude to be able to commit, then reap the rewards by doing it easily, laughingly and lovingly.

If you've got the magnetism of chemistry, the generosity of abundant love and the maturity of commitment, congratulate yourselves and celebrate your relationship. You deserve it.

Now that we've underlined the importance of commitment, let's talk some more about it.

'I'm Here Aren't I?' ... Dealing with the 'C' Word

The question I get asked most frequently as a relationship therapist is, 'What is the most prevalent cause of relationship breakdown?' The answer is, unequivocally, lack of commitment. The most widely requested definition is for the concept of commitment, and I have therefore devised the following:

1. Commitment is not a concept, it is an experience, as real as riding a bicycle. If you don't know whether you're committed or not, you're not. You'll know when you are.
2. There are no degrees of commitment. Commitment is an absolute, like a light switch with no dimmers: *on* or *off*. There's no such thing as being a *little* committed or *very* committed, only *totally* committed.

So, what is commitment?
1. A commitment is what you make to someone you choose freely because of a deep sense that this person is the one for you. Don't get into a relationship for any reason or need, because once you've satisfied the reason or need, there's no longer any reason or need for the relationship.

2.   Commitment is made in the spirit of *forever.*

3.   Commitment means there's a neon sign flashing across your forehead which reads *not available* for anything that will defer, deflect or diminish the relationship with the person to whom you've committed.

4.   Commitment means that when required you can be selfless enough to make your partner's needs more important than your own. The only people who can do this are those who have a solid grasp of who they are, are sure they can get their own needs met and, most importantly, know how to stay *true to themselves.*

5.   Being committed means that the truth for you is that in your heart, in your mind, in private and in public your behaviour makes the statement that you are unequivocally your partner's man or woman.

6.   Commitment calls for your ego to be less important to you than your partner's need to tell you how upset they feel about something you've done, even if this entails having to be wrong or feeling like an idiot.

7.   In other words, commitment involves loving your partner so much that in being able to make their needs more important than your own, you are occasionally willing to be in a state of discomfort. It is important this sense of sacrifice is reciprocal.

8.   Commitment can end with integrity if you've done all of the above 100 per cent but the person to whom you've committed requires that you compromise your real self.

9.   At times, commitment is a hard slog and a downright pain in the bum.

10.   The ability to commit puts you on a higher plane. Only a

small percentage of the population is capable of commitment (mostly because of number 4).

Statistically, men have a more difficult time with commitment than women, so, men, let's have a good look at you, and why this should be so.

Getting Men Wrong

In America, women's call to arms was heralded by Gloria Steinem in the late 1960s: 'A man is to a woman as a bicycle is to a goldfish.' Those were the words that rang out across the land. And thousands of us raised our hands in unison and said, 'Right on, Gloria, right on!'

I'd never thought about whether the men in my life were necessary or not necessary. My father had marched off to war to fight for peace, justice and the American way. Of course I had him on a pedestal. I was raised in a television era where, once a week, Robert Young would come into my living room in *Father Knows Best* and prove yet again that, indeed, this was the case.

So what made me take up the call so easily? I think it was the cleverness of those words. As unnecessary 'as a bicycle is to a goldfish'? How could words so clever, so sarcastic, so cheeky and revolutionary not be true? So now I, along with thousands of my sisters, developed the mandatory mild disdain and smug superiority towards a gender for whom previously I had obsolutely no axe to grind.

Two things changed that. First, I moved to Australia and fell in love with the Australian male's rugged individualism and no-nonsense masculinity — and subsequently married one. Trust me. He has no time for anyone's mild disdain or smug superiority. Secondly, I hung out my psychologist's shingle. Anyone who has ever hung out a shingle knows that you take whatever shows up and are grateful. Surprisingly and predominantly, what showed up were men.

Thus started a long affair with the male psyche. It compelled me to navigate unknown waters. It made me think, understand and translate in a language that was not my mother tongue. Increasingly, what developed was an uneasy sense that maybe, just maybe, they've been terribly maligned. Concurrently, I began to develop a creeping crankiness with the women's movement. I have four issues I wish to bring up.

1. Fundamentally, I feel that the philosophy of the women's movement was founded on a false premise. The mistake we made was taking men personally. We thought their behaviour was aimed at us, but it isn't. Men also do what they do to each other, it's what they do to everyone.

In the professional world, men are competitive and power-driven. It's as true and instinctive in human males as in males in the animal kingdom. They jostle to become leader of the pack. In their striving to attain that goal, they have a 'take no prisoners' mentality. Some men do this nicely, à la Dick Smith, and some do it in a megalomaniacal J. R. Ewing way. But the end result is the same — the weak are left behind.

Women at the top are now being accused of the same aggressive, power-driven behaviour. They've learned. If you're going to make it in a man's game, you've got to play by men's rules. It's the way it works. And it's nothing personal.

In the relationship world, women complain that men are out of touch with their emotions, that they're insensitive and lack the ability to commit or be intimate with us. Take a look at how men relate to each other. The reason why mateship works so well is because of the rules. Most men don't spend a lot of time thinking about their emotions, but not necessarily because they avoid them. Instead, emotionally, they're more apt to just get on with it.

A lot of men don't take criticism as personally as women. Men don't require or ask for intimacy with each other, so no-one ever gets let down. And as for commitment, they know that when they get on each other's nerves, it's perfectly all right to take a hike and come back when they feel like it, no questions asked.

Mateship is where men can fail at every requirement women ask of them, and still get to feel OK about themselves. This is my point, men do what they do. We made a mistake when we took them personally.

2. Back to Gloria Steinem. As clever as her war cry was, it simply isn't true. If a woman is heterosexual, and she has a sex drive, and she prefers human contact to plastic, she needs a man.

3. My third gripe is one that has developed with evolution. Twenty-five years ago we described the problem: 'Men aren't the way we need them to be.' Fair enough. Twenty-five years later we've come no further. We're still discussing the problem. No-one has yet provided the solution: 'If they do the following

things, they will be the way we need them to be.' Is that because we're too stupid to come up with answers, or because we're in love with the problem and, if we solved it, we'd have to give it up?

Because I have never met a stupid feminist, and because the women's movement is perceived by some to be prone towards self-righteousness, it makes one wonder if the latter is the answer. The movement often seems more about making men wrong than about getting our needs met.

The 'us' and 'them' mentality appears so evident that sometimes the unavoidable conclusion is that no matter how right 'they' got it, 'they' might not ever be OK because a lot of us just plain don't like 'them' and aren't about to, no matter what. Now that's all right, but we shouldn't tizzy it up with high-falutin moral superiority.

It's this victim mentality that really does women the most harm. In therapy, I teach women who are genuine about wanting to bridge the chasm that they have two choices. They can either hold onto whatever battle scars they have attributed to men in their lives, as evidence of what 'they did to me', or they can cash in their victim card and get their needs met. The sacrifice is, the s.o.b. back then, who 'did it', gets to walk off scot-free.

Although it's a tough trade-off, I see women do it all the time. To a liberated woman who has solved the problem of getting her needs met by the male in her life, and is co-existing with one, not only in harmony, but in true enhancement of her life, the movement has become outdated.

4.   Any cause that calls itself a 'woman's movement' surely

ought to be committed to the welfare of its membership, its platform dedicated to the eradication of the causes that oppress and the sources of pain for the people it represents. Where is feminism on the issue of the 'other woman'?

When I'm sitting in my rooms with a woman who is in a state of mental paralysis, who tells me breathing is hard, guess what she's not referring to? She's not alluding to sexual discrimination in the workplace. She's not talking about glass ceilings or equal pay.

Her complaint is that she and her three children have been violated by a predator called the 'other woman'. Where do we get off standing in moral superiority over men, when we haven't cleaned up the mess we cause each other? At least from where I'm standing, there's often more fraternity in mateship than there is sorority in the sisterhood. If we've got enemies, let's be fair dinkum about all of them.

All I know is that we're angrier, more self-righteous and more judgmental than our mothers. In one generation we've moved from being door-mats to penis loppers. And men are close to becoming crippled, apologetic, politically correct, jibbering robots. They've got no idea who to be.

There's an exception to all of this. There are women who are smart enough to pick the eyes out of the movement and make it work for them. Starting with 'men aren't the way we need them to be', what these women did was to become very clear and focused on the way they needed the men in their lives to be, in order for their relationships to work.

They're women who are willing to take responsibility for the way they communicate with their men. They clearly state their needs. If that fails, they negotiate. If that fails, they set uncompromisable limits. If that fails, they're willing to get out, to walk away. What these women have in common is they're not judgmental. They're not stuck in the problem. They insist their relationships are win–win. They like men and their focus is on making it work.

And as for men, my experience is, they're not all bad. They hate hurting women, and they're eager to get it right. When a man says, 'All I want is for you to be happy,' why wouldn't he be genuine? Considering what he gets when we're not happy, he'd be mad to mean anything less.

Let's move on towards bridging the gap — here's a road map to better understanding.

Getting Men Right

Let's face it — relationships are in a mess. At least they are if one believes the statistics. I'm aware statistics can be used to push a certain point of view, but the view from where I'm sitting, as a relationship therapist, is that relationships *are* in a mess. So I thought I'd try to make a contribution towards bridging the gap that exists between the sexes and seems to be becoming a chasm.

Towards this cause, I'm willing to tell secrets from the old girls' club, which may well get me kicked out. For starters, understanding women is an oxymoron. We're complex, we're introspective and we're hormonally phasal. Sigmund Freud threw up his hands and bewailed, 'Women, what do they want? My God, what do they want?' His answer was a bit left field, chucking us all under the diagnosis of 'penis envy', but it certainly indicates the level of the man's frustration. We're not easy.

What's easy to understand are men. First of all, they're simple. I'm not saying dumb, I'm saying delightfully, uncomplicatedly, artlessly simple. They say what they *think* they mean and because they believe it, they mean what they say (with one exception which I'll go into later, and will call 'the exception'). Male simplicity is a problem for us because we're so different.

Often, when a man says something to us, we say to ourselves, 'He can't *really* mean that. He must have meant ...' and then we go into what *we* would have meant. He'll say, 'I'm not interested in a commitment.' We know that can't possibly be what he *really* means. Surely he wants a commitment. Deep down inside everybody wants a commitment *(because we do)*.

We assume it must have something to do with his mother or a previous girlfriend who let him down. We hang in there for ten years to prove that we're different from his mother and all his previous relationships. Then he'll realise what emptiness exists in his heart because he hasn't made a commitment. Ten years later we'll broach the subject and he'll say, 'I really love you. You're different from all my previous girlfriends and you're nothing like my mother, but I don't want a commitment.' When men say things, we should believe them. There's usually no hidden agenda. It's what they mean.

'The exception': the other thing about men is pretty quirky. They seem to have a pathological disorder (this being the term I give to anything I can't otherwise explain). Men have a pathological need to be right. I have never understood why *no matter what* a man *cannot* ask for directions. A pathological need to be right explains that.

If one matches up 'they mean what they say' with 'pathological need to be right', what we can get is the following scenario: he's told us that he doesn't want a commitment. And we know he can't *really* mean that. We wait it out for the ten years. We finally give up and get out of the relationship. There's every likelihood that within a week he could be married to someone he met the day after we left. He meant what he said to *us* and needed to stay 'right' about it. If he says he doesn't want a commitment, believe him and save ten years.

The next thing that's good to know about men is what their favourite thing is. A man's favourite thing is to be adored. Women assume their favourite thing is sex. Men *need* sex, but they get more ego gratification and self-esteem from being adored.

Another reality is that men are naughty. I think they'd have no problem admitting they do some pretty naughty things. They're more instinct-motivated than women. The good news is they don't mind being stopped. In fact, I think that, for a man, respect for a woman is largely predicated on knowing he's met his match, knowing she'll not let him get away with bad behaviour.

I have a client who came to me because he couldn't make up his mind between his girlfriend and his wife. In the end he chose the girlfriend. This is why: he wasn't committed to his wife and complained she had a 'victim mentality'. He despised the 'tread here' sign she seemed to have stamped across her forehead. She was always in pain about something he'd done, so around her he always felt bad about himself. This made him resent her and provoked him to treat her with a lack of respect.

The girlfriend wouldn't put up with any such nonsense. She gave him an ultimatum about his intentions and about his marriage. He said that in the end he decided on the girlfriend because she insisted he treat her well. He liked who he was around her, she made him feel good about himself.

Finally, men love to be acknowledged for what they consider to be their contribution. They like to know that what they do for us makes a difference to the quality of our lives. They don't need to believe we wouldn't exist if they weren't around, but that our life is much better with them in it.

Back to relationships being in a mess.

1.   About men being *simple*. I've already said that we have a hard time stopping ourselves from translating what men say into female language, with its attendant meanings, i.e. into what we would hear if we were saying the same thing. This creates huge communication hassles.

2.   About men wanting to be *adored*. We've done nothing else for twenty-five years but let them know that, unequivocally, in our opinion, they're lower than a snake's belly. It's about time we lightened up.

3.   About men being *naughty*. For millennia women have demonstrated that we chalk up greater self-righteousness mileage making men wrong than by getting our needs met, i.e. 'If you don't know what the matter is, then don't worry about it!'

4.   About *acknowledging men for their contribution*. Our catch-cry for the last twenty-five years has been, 'I can do it *myself*, thank you very much!' Or else we let them know in no uncertain terms that whatever their contribution is, either it's not the one we want, or we could do it better.

Maybe, just maybe, if we stopped shouting, 'If you *really* loved me you'd know what my needs are and fulfil them the way I want you to. What kind of a person can't get that right?' for five seconds, and took a look at where men are coming from, we'd start making our relationships win–win situations. My observation is that a well-loved man is willing to do practically *anything* for his partner.

I'm not saying we need to get obsequious or soppy. I'm saying that as much as we need to soften up, we also need to become a lot more focused about getting our needs met. In the naughty behaviour department, we need to learn to say *that's enough!!* We need to know we are capable of setting limits, and that if our partner insists on stepping over those limits, we're prepared and capable enough to get out of the relationship, *no matter what.*

What we need to do is to get smarter. Wisdom means knowing the difference between being right and winning. The price for being right is:

1. Our looks. We look angry, judgmental, self-righteous and hard done by.

2. Our relationships. For every relationship that a man walks out of, what you'll see is his new partner looking at him as if she were witnessing the second coming of Christ. (Often these relationships don't last. Either because she's insincere — although a smart player — or he gets real.) I'm not advocating artificial or exaggerated behaviour, but there is a clue in it.

Winning means getting off our soapboxes, lightening up and getting our sense of humour back. The rewards for winning are:

1. Our looks. We can start looking confident, approachable and loving.

2. Our relationships. Through expressing our love for our partners, we can fall in love with ourselves. We get in touch

with the power we have to make a difference to someone else's life. 'Hey, *I* put that look on his face.' We can then feel valued, looked after, loved. And by setting limits we get to have our needs met, to strengthen our self-esteem and to know what respect really feels like.

A challenge to women: make a resolution that for the next week you'll attempt to acknowledge one male a day for something positive he's done. It has to be honest, no tokenism. Notice what happens. See if it comes easily or if it's difficult. Take note of what you get back in return (after he checks to see if you're fair dinkum).

I have a client who after doing this exercise lost 10 kilos. She stopped needing to use her overweight body to prove how men have never loved her for her real self. She started to see that it was her anger at *them* that caused her to use her body as evidence of how badly treated she thought she'd been.

By understanding men and behaving accordingly, if nothing else, at least women can start to make a contribution towards cleaning up the relationship mess.

Of course, understanding someone doesn't mean you automatically get your needs met. It helps to have communication skills, and to master the art of negotiation.

How to Negotiate and Win

After all these years of being in practice, you'd think I'd get used to the question. I don't. When people ask me how long therapy takes, the answer is that it depends on how long it takes to tell your story. You may think I'm referring to how fast a person can talk, but I'm not.

What I mean is, it depends on how long it takes to get the story out of your system. For some people that takes forever — which is expensive. But some people really need to know that I understand their point of view. They want me to agree that they are the 'right' party, that they're the wrongly done by partner. When I attempt to drag them back on track by asking them what they're in therapy for, it reminds them. It's to fix a broken relationship. Funny how often being right is more important to some people than fixing the problem.

I'm still amazed that when someone finally finishes their story (because they no longer have any oxygen), I can ask them what they *want* and they look at me as though I've just broken into pidgin English. How can someone have a broken relationship and *not know what they want*? It happens all the time. If you're ready to stop telling the story and start mending a broken relationship, or making a good relationship even better, here's some advice.

1. *Communicate.*

Ask yourself some questions. Which need isn't being met? What is it your partner is doing that is upsetting you? How long has it been going on? When did you first notice it? Are you angry? Why haven't you spoken up? Are you blaming your partner for not knowing what's bothering you? Are you willing to be accountable for your resentment? (They do something that drives you nuts but you don't tell them what that is; and every time they do it you deem yourself justified in feeling homicidal inclinations towards them. Not very nice.)

When you're ready to be responsible for your resentment, then take all of the judgment out of your message and communicate it. It's best if you use 'I' statements: 'I would love it if you'd clean up the dishes after you have a snack.' 'I need you to stop flirting with other people at parties.' 'When you criticise me a lot, it makes me feel inadequate. I'd appreciate it if you'd stop.'

Turning up the heat, if the above fails:

2. *Negotiate.*

The following is a three-part negotiating technique:

(a) Talk to yourself about what you want to negotiate. You need to ask yourself, 'What do I want? What do I need?' When you're quite clear about your answer, you need to get it down to a paragraph. After that, get it down to a sentence. Now get it down to no more than ten words. You can slip past a person's defence mechanisms if you get in and out in under ten words.

(b) Pick your time and place. You want a successful outcome. So bow to your partner's biorhythms. If your partner is a night person tackle the negotiation in the afternoon or evening, if they are a morning person talk to them in the morning. Don't interrupt if they're in the middle of something special. You want their mind to be at optimal availability. And never negotiate around alcohol.

(c) You need an exit line. The exit line should be pre-rehearsed, come in the form of a question and involve a total change of subject. The purpose of an exit line is to let your partner know the topic is closed, the sky hasn't fallen in, everybody's OK and now it's time to get on with life. The first part of the sentence is a non-negotiable statement of need. It doesn't call for a response, just compliance. The second part softens the blow; a bitter pill washed down with a lolly.

For example: the time and place are right. You have your partner's maximum mind availability, and you are about to communicate something that addresses the issue of 'What I want is . . .' Here goes: 'Please clean up your own dishes, and which movie do you want to watch tonight?' Or, 'Don't criticise me and do you want red or white wine with the chicken?' Or, 'I need you to stop flirting at parties, and is it cold enough to need a jumper?'

Here are some potential snags. Your partner comes back with a rejoinder like, 'I only criticise you when you deserve it.' You need to stay focused on the purpose of the negotiation, which is to get your need met. 'This is not a discussion. I don't want you to criticise me again, and you haven't answered the question. Do you want red or white?'

The other pitfall to watch out for is the tendency to want to explain and justify your request, like: 'The reason I hate you criticising me is because it makes both of us look stupid in the eyes of our friends.'

'There you go, always worrying about what other people think.' Every word you use over and above the basic statement of your need can and will be used as a boomerang. Trust me. Ten words is a good guideline.

Turning up the heat, if the above fails:

3. *Set Limits.*

The rehearsal for this is best done in an isolated spot where no-one can hear you, perhaps when there's no-one else home, or in your car with the windows shut. What you need to repeat over and over again is, *'Don't you ever, ever, ever do that to me again.'* Get angry. Get good, clean, healthy, adrenalin-pumping angry. Start to feel very entitled.

When you're ready the two words to deliver are: *That's enough!!!* It helps if you bend your elbow aiming your index finger in the direction of their chest. It helps to maintain eye contact until they look away or it's clear the point has been served and received. It helps if you can speak from your solar plexus.

Turning up the heat, if the above fails:

4. *Get Out.*

I don't mean for an hour or for the afternoon. I mean walk away from the relationship. My only advice on this is to wait until you're ready, really ready. If you do this prematurely, you'll only come back in order to pretend that something is OK that clearly is not OK. Save yourself the time and drama. When you're ready, walk away forever.

Ultimately, our responsibility in our life and particularly in our relationships, is to get our needs met. If we don't get our needs met, at worst, we emotionally starve to death. At best, we go around feeling resentful, negative, accusatory and ripped off. Our lives are not a charity. If people are constantly draining our cup, we end up with nothing to give. Our first obligation is to fill our cup so we can afford to donate to others from a reality of abundance. Being able to be intimate with your partner is one way of getting your cup filled.

How Are You, How Are You *Really?*

There's an old Indian saying, 'In order to know a man, you have to walk a mile in his moccasins.' What becomes more and more apparent is that in order for a man to know a woman he needs to walk a mile in her party shoes. Then he needs to know what muscles hurt, how badly and where they need to be rubbed.

A lack of ability to be intimate is frustrating. It's soul-destroying for the partner who is being denied it. It's frustrating for me because I find it so hard to teach. Explaining intimacy is like trying to pick up the mercury from a broken thermometer. Just when you think you've got your finger on it, it runs away from you. When I think I've got a workable definition, I'll get asked a 'How do you do it?' question that calls for turning concept into experience and I'm lost. How do you explain the flavour chocolate?

Generally speaking, intimacy inadequacy is, more often than not, a male affliction. I'm not exactly sure why, but the male world is more fact, business and materially focused. The female world tends to be more relationship, nurturing and feelings oriented. Caring, tending and mothering calls for intimacy. A male can go to his grave a so-called 'successful person' without it. Mateship doesn't call for intimacy, nor does sport, nor does the workplace. But if he wants a successful relationship with a woman, he must master it.

Here's how it worked for Robert and Elizabeth.

Robert has been separated from his wife for six years. Four years ago he met Elizabeth and they became mutually besotted. Robert promised Elizabeth he'd start instituting divorce proceedings, he 'just hadn't gotten around to it yet'. Two years passed and Robert still hadn't taken the first step. Elizabeth went into therapy.

As a result of therapy, and Elizabeth's newly found feelings of self-worth and entitlement, she broke off her relationship with Robert. This gave Robert enough of a fright to induce him to promise her the moon and hire a divorce lawyer. They reunited. I don't know whether Robert is ambivalent, uncommitted or lazy, but after the reunion, he became semi-inert again.

Elizabeth was booked in for an appointment and I was to see Robert an hour later. Elizabeth was a mess. She'd lost weight and had dark circles under her eyes. She explained that when she tried to discuss the issue or start to back out of the relationship, Robert would either yell at her for being on his back, that he was doing the best he could do, or he'd book them another trip to Europe and another appointment with his lawyer. But the proceedings were still crawling along at a snail's pace. She explained that she was no longer angry so much as emotionally devasted. The issue was no longer Robert's divorce as much as it was his lack of concern about her well-being.

Robert's turn. He looked exasperated. 'How's it going, Robert?'

'This relationship is no longer fun! I've had Elizabeth up to the back teeth! All she does is nag, nag, nag! I'm doing the best I can! These things don't happen overnight! Why can't she understand that?'

'Robert, you're obviously upset. Tell me everything that's on your plate. Give me a list of everything in your life that's a worry.'

'Well, work is stressful. The deadlines don't let up. This divorce business is a hassle. It eats into my time. But the most frustrating thing in my life is the pressure of Elizabeth. She doesn't let up. Now I'm getting that "biological time-clock" crap!'

'Is that it? Anything else on the list?'

'I think that's enough for one man.'

'Robert, do you love Elizabeth?'

'What an insane question. Do you think I'd go through all this if I didn't love her?'

'Do you think that you know Elizabeth?'

'I know her better than she knows herself.'

'How is she?'

'Distraught. She's worked herself up into a real state.'

'Robert, do you realise that you've enumerated your list of mental concerns, everything that's on your mind, and the fact that the woman you love, that you want to marry and look after, is an emotional wreck, is not even on the list?

'She isn't nearly as upset about the divorce as she is about the fact that she can't get through to you that the mess she's in is caused by your lack of care about her distress. What she feels so upset about is very hurtful for her, but because it's not hurtful for you, her anguish is what you're calling "pressure" and a pain in the neck for you.'

'Pretend that you have a really close friend and he punches you in the face, and that causes you to yell in pain. Now your friend gets furious at you for yelling. You not only have to deal with the hurt of a close friend inflicting pain on you, but you also have the problem of your friend being inconvenienced by your reaction to him hurting you. When you try to explain how you feel, he rolls his eyes, accuses you of pressuring him and tells you to shut up.'

A very dark cloud of understanding is coming over Robert.

Elizabeth comes into the room. 'Elizabeth, I'm so sorry. I'm really, really sorry.'

Robert's first act of intimacy.

Intimacy starts with acute listening. It's completed with the ability to convey successfully to your partner that you've received, understood and empathised with what they've said. It calls for concentrating on knowing who your partner is and what they're communicating to you, both verbally and non-verbally. If you were in business and your career depended on a certain client, it would behove you to know them intimately. Successful hunters know their prey intimately. Mechanics know engines intimately.

The problem with intimacy in relationships is that sometimes what your partner is communicating is that the strife they are in is being caused by you. If they were upset with the next-door neighbour, it wouldn't be a problem. The characteristics of people who aren't good at intimacy are defensiveness, unconsciousness and the inability to be wrong. In order to be intimate, your partner's emotional needs have to be more important to you than your own ego.

It's hard to see someone you care about in pain, under any circumstances. The reason it's hard is because if you let in what they are feeling, you feel their pain. It's a thousand times harder when you're feeling their pain and knowing that the pain you're both feeling has been caused by you. What helps is making sure that you pick a partner who is special enough to be worth the discomfort. The reward is in knowing you are big enough to be capable of nurturing, caring and being intimate with someone you love.

That Couldn't Happen to Me

Denial is nature's little way of providing the mind with a reality valve, an escape hatch. Denial is what makes parents disbelieve their child cheated in the maths exam. Denial is what makes losing punters know the next horse will be the one. It's what allows people to smoke. And it's why people stay in bad relationships.

The mind can only take in so much before it switches to overload. Denial allows us to shut off and not take in any more. Denial is a trickster that can allow us to fool ourselves into believing what suits us at the time.

Peter and Rachael have been in a de facto relationship for twelve years. Rachael would like to get married. She hopes that if she just stays patient, Peter will come around to the idea.

My client was Rachael's best friend. Her problem was that Peter made a play for her. She didn't take it personally. Peter made a play for other female friends as well.

My client had no problem with Peter. She liked him and was able to handle the situation. Her problem was Rachael. My client was paralysed by indecision. She had never revealed the truth to Rachael. She said her reason was that Rachael was the most perceptive person about other people that she had ever known. She couldn't fathom why Rachael didn't know what others knew. She interpreted a vibe Rachael put out that made her avoid the subject. She valued their relationship and she wanted my advice.

I have always maintained, in my personal life, that I am not the reality police. If a friend asks a question, I will accept that as an invitation to reply, no matter how brutal the answer. But I do not feed unsolicited information to people. It is my observation that on an unconscious level, everyone knows everything. In nearly twenty years of infidelity counselling, I have only had one wife who swears she had no idea, on any level, that any treachery was going on. I respect a person's right to deal with information on a conscious level at their rate of readiness, not mine.

One day, the inevitable happened. Peter made the mistake of hitting on a new friend of Rachael's, an ardent feminist. She told Rachael.

Rachael confronted my client. 'Did you know?' My client admitted she did and reflected my point of view. Rachael's answer was standard: 'And you call yourself a friend!' It's a predicament all of us have faced at one time or another.

The short-term story was hard. Rachael said she felt betrayed by my client and refused to talk to her. My client explained that she was acting out of an instinctive care for Rachael's psychological well-being. Although she was sorry about what Rachael was dealing with, she would have done the same thing again. She told Rachael that she respected whatever Rachael needed to do to cope with what was going on. She would be there for her whenever she was ready.

Three months later Rachael contacted my client. She said my client had read it right. Deep down she did know what Peter was up to, but she also knew that he wasn't committed to her. She knew if she had allowed herself to be conscious of his activity, she would have had to confront him. She was afraid he would have left her and she couldn't have handled that. She was too afraid to take the gamble.

Rachael gained enough self-esteem to establish that she was entitled to be with a man who respected her enough to be faithful and committed to her. She became ready and able to confront Peter. All or nothing. The fact that Rachael valued herself enough to demand that his behaviour change became the catalyst for him to respect her enough to comply.

Would Rachael have had it out with Peter earlier if my client had confronted her with the truth? She would probably have refused to believe it or pretended it didn't matter. The reason that Rachael didn't confront Peter earlier was not because she didn't have sufficient information. It was because she wasn't ready to deal with her fear of being alone, of being without Peter.

If my client had told her earlier, Rachael may have avoided her for longer. There would have been a piece of information hanging, out loud, in the air between the two of them that Rachael was incapable of handling. Every time they were together, their meeting would have confronted Rachael with what she was unable to face and rectify.

Denial is a good and bad thing. If taken too far, it can turn reality into delusion or fantasy. This isn't good. At some point we all have to deal appropriately with what is on our plates, in order to get on with our lives and not get stuck in one place.

On the other hand, denial can come in handy. Sometimes we may be headed in a certain direction that is important to us. Information may come in that is so overwhelming that if we let it in, it would totally interrupt our process, purpose or goal. 'I'll deal with that later' or 'I've put it temporarily in the too-hard basket' can be an energy and focus saver. Parents save telling bad news to higher school certificate sitters until the exam is over for this reason. Things put in the too-hard basket are only in storage, they don't disappear. Eventually they need to be taken out and dealt with.

Avoid denying being in denial. Acknowledge there is an outstanding issue you aren't ready to look at. This beats pretending you don't know the issue exists.

'Ready' is the operative word. We don't deal with the matter because we aren't ready and we will deal with it when we are. This helps take the issue out of the never-never. It respects the need for a mind in overload to have a holiday. It also strengthens the intention to get a shelved matter dealt with appropriately upon return.

Speaking of things that are hard to face, there are some issues that are certainly harder to deal with than others.

Sharks in the Water

Message on my answering machine: 'Please call Barbara Smith.'

'Hi, Barbara. What can I do for you?'

'I don't know what to do.'

'About what?'

'It's 9.00 a.m., I'm in bed and I literally don't know what I'm supposed to do after my feet hit the floor.'

There is only one situation I know of that evokes that kind of paralysis — Barbara's husband, Ian, has left her for another woman.

I'm not banging my own drum here. I personally have never been the other woman's victim, but I deal with them for a living, and their pain gets to me.

The other woman is usually damaged goods. What I mean by this is that somewhere in her past there is a man who did something to her. Some man has hurt her badly. What she's concluded is that when it comes to men, in the end they always let you down.

The worst part of the let-down was that the pain inflicted

was out of their control. The life's decision they make is that they will never be hurt again by something out of their control. The only way to be in control of being hurt is to pick a partner who will most likely end up hurting them. So, when it happens, they are in pain, but not shocked, surprised or wrong about their hypothesis that in the end, all men are bastards.

Often the function of the other woman is to serve as a passion partner in a marriage that's going through a flat period. Every fire has its blaze, but in the end it cools into reality. Once the married man comes up for air, often what he sees is that he's being unrealistic. What he's fallen in love with is falling in love. He's trading one set of problems for another.

'My wife doesn't understand me' and *Snow White* are fairy tales. What he's really saying is that he doesn't understand what commitment means. 'We don't have a sex life.' Often that's not true; if it is true, the other woman's function is to be a solution.

If the married man is available to the other woman, that means he's not committed to his wife. In other words, he can be got. If he can be got by *this* other woman, then he can be got by another other woman.

In the reception line of a wedding where the other woman had won, she whispered in my ear, 'I got him from Sarah. I wonder who will get him from me?' Happy wedding! Why would anyone walk wide-eyed into a relationship fraught with so much danger?

The answer is they are damaged people. If a fair dinkum fellow showed up, who knew what commitment meant and was available for it, the other woman wouldn't be interested.

She'd say one of two things: 'He doesn't turn me on sexually because he's too wimpy' or 'He's boring.' You see, if she met a real relationship contender and he asked her to trust him, and she did, and he hurt her, she'd be hurt *and* out of control.

As for Barbara, she slowly rediscovered what to do when her feet hit the floor, one step at a time. By staying realistic about Ian's inability to be committed and monogamous, she started to see him as weak. She lost respect for him as a man. She's now happily dating a man who thinks she's Christmas. She's moved on.

As for Ian, he quit therapy because he thought I was too harsh in my personality profile of t.o.w. (the other woman). He claimed she was an exception to my warning. A year later, he's heavily into damage control about what he's lost and horrified by comparisons between the woman he left behind and the possessiveness and insecurity of the woman he thought was the love of his life.

The hook the other woman has is her story about how badly she's been treated by men. Every man wants to prove that he's the exception to her rule. He'll show her he's the real knight on the steed who will prove her wrong. He'll be her saviour and hero. In the beginning, she'll let him be that. This is intoxicating stuff for men.

The wife can't compete with the pedestal t.o.w. has put him on. The wife's love for him is less heady, more realistic. It includes history, career anxiety, ups and downs, success and failure, financial worry, children, stress and dirty socks. T.o.w. offers 'clean slate' love.

What the husband doesn't understand is that often the

hero worship love that got him in is short-lived. It can last until she actually lands him. The agony that t.o.w. goes through until she gets him allows her to remain true to her conviction that men spell pain. She never gets to wake up in the morning with the man she loves. She spends weekends and holidays alone. His children *always* come first.

Remember, in order for the other woman to continue to see the husband as a hero she has to cash in her entire belief system about men. Now that she actually has him, her issues will turn into issues other than 'when is he going to leave his wife?' Now she becomes a textbook case of insecurity: 'You still love your wife,' 'Your children are more important to you than I am,' 'Your love isn't as intense as when we were courting,' 'You spend more money on your first family than on me.' No matter what, no matter how hard he tries, she will never let him be OK in her book.

In order for him to get out of the relationship, he's going to have to cop her believing he's just one more bastard in a long line of bastards. That's a long drop from seeing himself as a white knight! This ploy keeps men in relationships long past their use-by date.

I'm not saying men are off the hook regarding responsibility in this issue. But it seems to me that when it comes to a contest of flirtation and seduction, even men of high resolve, historically, come off second best. Just ask Adam.

The solution is threefold:

1. Wives, take heed. There are sharks in the water. Don't take your husbands for granted. A little acknowledgment goes a long way. If you make him out to be wrong a lot, there are plenty of

women out there who will make him feel right about himself.

2. Husbands, grow up. There's an experience out there waiting to be discovered that feels bigger and better than the need for hero worship. It's called commitment.

3. Other women, aside from what you're doing to the rest of the cast of characters, take a good, hard look at what you're doing to yourselves. You're ripping youselves off. If a married man shows interest in you, tell him to come back when the ink is dry on his divorce papers. Get some good counselling. Stop settling for a slice. There are whole pies going.

I'll Have
What They're
Having

I'm going to be perfectly honest. There are some things that are easier for a therapist to treat than others, namely, things the therapist has experienced first-hand. There are a couple of problems that come my way where commonsense has to prevail, because, in terms of personal experience, I'm flying blind.

One is the issue of jealousy. On that one, what I've done is try to analyse why I don't feel jealousy. The people who come to talk about the problem don't want to feel jealous, so I explain why I feel the way I do. This seems to help navigate a course towards an alternative way to react. You wouldn't exactly want to refer them to a jealousy-afflicted therapist, because from where I'm standing jealousy makes people look and act nuts.

Basically, between envy, covetousness and jealousy what we're talking about is, 'I want something someone else has. I'm afraid someone will get what I have. I don't want someone to have what they have, if I can't have what they have.' What it looks like is someone walking down the street with a really sour look on their face, when there's a good chance their best friend just won the lottery.

There are two reasons why I have never experienced jealousy in a relationship. One is that either my partner is doing the wrong thing by me or he's not. Worrying about it isn't going to alter whether he is or he isn't. Yes, I'd want to know if something was going on. But why ruin a good thing until, and if, it's necessary? I'd rather live in a fool's paradise. I can afford to do this because when and if I find out I've been wrong, I'm confident that, aside from looking silly, I'll be able to handle it at that time. The by-product of behaving this way is it allows a lot of spontaneity and freedom for my partner. Somehow I feel that contributes to why he doesn't do the wrong thing by me.

The second reason I don't feel jealousy is that I don't feel my partner should ever feel beholden to me. If he wants to get out of the relationship because he prefers someone else, I couldn't stand him staying with me out of charity. I'm not saying it wouldn't hurt, it would be terrible, but partnership through obligation would be worse. It would be humiliating and degrading.

In relationships where there is a jealous partner the object of the jealousy is always in the doghouse, whether they are guilty or innocent. They have the feeling of being a condemned person. Often the experience of never being trusted by the jealous partner feels like defeat; like never scoring a win or never feeling good about yourself.

I had a client who was undyingly faithful. He was determined to prove to his untrusting partner that she had nothing to fear, he'd never hurt her. After years of never being acknowledged for his fidelity and sensitivity, and constantly being questioned, disbelieved and checked up on, he started to become resentful. When an opportunity showed up that was tempting, he decided, 'The hell with it', and went ahead and had the fling. How many times have I heard, 'As long as I'm going to be accused of it anyway, I might as well do it.'

This man admitted the other woman meant nothing to him, he was just frustrated and angry. The other thing he said was he was lonely in his marriage. He never felt he was being related to as his real self. His wife always related to him as if he were permanently cast in the role of the deceitful pain inflicter.

He told me he had no problem trusting himself not to cheat again because monogamy had never been a problem for him. His act in many ways was more an act of vindictiveness than of infidelity. He said he found his wife's jealousy suffocating and he wouldn't consider staying married unless she could control it.

In working with his wife, what became apparent was that the function of her jealousy was to maintain control. It was almost like a superstition. As long as she suspected him of doing the wrong thing, she would never have to be vulnerable to the hurt she would feel if she trusted him and *then* he let her down. What she began to see was that it didn't work. Not only was she hurt anyway, but it was her mistrust that, in part, caused her fear to become a self-fulfilling prophecy.

What she realised was you can't control relationships. They're a risk for all of us. If your partner does the wrong thing, you're going to be hurt. There's no escaping it. You can only decide whether you can afford to be hurt and survive it or not.

If you can't, then you shouldn't be in a relationship. Or you should wait until you can afford to be at risk.

My client decided her husband really was a good man, she really did love him, and it was worth the gamble. Since she survived this time, she'd survive if it ever happened again. In the 'old habits die hard' category, I suggested that she was probably still going to have feelings of insecurity for a while. That's OK, but she needs to have them responsibly. They're her problem, and her husband shouldn't have to suffer because of them. She said she could handle that. Happy ending.

This form of jealousy is called the 'I'm afraid someone will get what I have' form of jealousy.

Jealousy can be a pretty serious business. There's a condition called 'obsessive jealousy disorder'. This is an affliction whereby the sufferer has such a strong identification with the object of their attention that, in a way, their two personalities become one. They see the other person as being part of themself. If they lose the other person, they experience feelings of panic because part of themself feels like it's disappearing.

Alan, who suffers from this disorder, loves Mary. In his mind, Mary now 'has' him. Mary stops loving Alan and goes away. Alan feels like she's taken him away with her. Mary now falls in love with Keith. Alan feels that, through Mary, he's being shared with another man. The feelings of lack of control are intolerable.

In extreme cases, the sufferer can hear voices. If their partner picks up some of their behaviour patterns (as two people in long-term relationships often do), they can feel as though those behaviours are stolen and they can no longer own them. The partner becomes very powerful and threatening to them.

This is a serious condition and should be treated seriously. The sufferer should seek psychiatric help. There is medication that can greatly reduce the symptoms, and make the person feel much calmer and more able to cope. Their partner should try to be empathetic, recognise that the person has an affliction and try not to take their behaviour personally. Be sympathetic, as you would to anyone with a medical complaint. You need to be supportive and to encourage your partner to receive professional help.

On the other hand, it is imperative that you take all precautions to protect yourself. If you've been threatened or treated violently, you must report this to the police. Even if you don't press charges, they should be on the alert, in case they are needed quickly. Contact your local community health service to see what their procedures are and find out if there are any emergency shelters in your vicinity. Don't let your pride be more important than your safety.

The form of jealousy that knocks my socks off is the one about not wanting someone to have what they have if I can't have what they have.

Ron and Yasmine are husband and wife. They lived in Perth. Ron was offered a job promotion if he was prepared to move to Melbourne. He and his wife discussed it and decided he should go first and suss it out, so Ron went ahead. He inherited Lisa, the secretary of his predecessor, and was dependent on her to help him learn the ropes. He was lonely. Lisa offered the solution. They had an affair.

The time comes for Yasmine to join Ron. Lisa looks after Yasmine. She shows her around the city and helps her to settle in. Yasmine is grateful. After a work social function, Ron, Yasmine and Lisa have a drink together. Yasmine twigs that there has been something going on between Lisa and her husband. She accuses them. Everyone confesses, cries, apologises and Ron and Lisa swear it will never happen again. Yasmine eventually gets over the hurt. Their marriage settles down. The job becomes permanent. Yasmine goes back to Perth to sell up.

The night before Yasmine is to return to Melbourne, Lisa invites Ron out to dinner to thank him for being a good friend, confidant and boss. She insists on picking him up so he can have a drink and not have to worry about driving. Several bottles of wine later, Lisa drives Ron home. She asks if he would mind inviting her in for 'one for the road'. One thing leads to another and they end up in the sack. One last time, 'for old times' sake'.

At midnight Lisa drives home, calls Yasmine in Perth and says, 'When you get to Melbourne tomorrow, check between the mattress and the bedspring. If you find a handkerchief with the initial "L" on it, you'll know who it belongs to.'

(Just in case Lisa is reading this, Ron and Yasmine got some therapy. The affair put Ron in touch with how close he came to losing Yasmine and how much he loved her. Their relationship is thriving on Ron's new-found understanding of monogamy and commitment. It was a good reason to make a fresh start. She's pregnant. They're thrilled.)

It's hard to know how to advise the Lisas out there. The disease is called 'meanness of spirit'. It's the same disorder suffered by the person whose best friend won the lottery. The only thing that comes to mind is, get a life!

Sometimes though, making relationships work can be doubly hard — without another party being involved — if you have picked the wrong partner to start with.

Oh No!
I've Done It
Again

This is the story of Judy Bates (and many others). Judy was born into a Disney production. Her household looked like a cross between 'Little House On the Prairie' and 'The Waltons'. Every night seven-year-old Judy ran down the path to greet Dad at the picket fence. He'd swing her up onto his shoulders and carry her into the house, from which wafted odours of a roast and apple pie. After Dad read Judy a night-time story, she'd glide off into blissful slumber. That was until the day Judy came home to find her mother sobbing in the kitchen.

'What's the matter, Mum?'

'Dad's gone away and we'll never see him again.'

Judy knew that was crazy because even if Dad wasn't fussed about Mum, he was mad about her. He'd never leave *her*. It took about a week for the shock to set in. Dad was never coming back. Judy sobbed herself to sleep every night. Just before she'd doze off, she'd vow, 'When I grow up, I'll never, ever be with a man who could abandon me.'

Fate was kind to Judy. She was blessed with good looks, intelligence, a sense of humour and compassion for her fellow human beings. She could probably have pointed to any male on the planet and said, 'I'll have you' and he would have said, 'Thank you.' The extraordinary thing is that Judy reached thirty having had eleven significant relationships. In every one of them, she got dropped from a great height. Each was a complete disaster.

The eleventh man has just walked out the door and Judy is feeling like death. She decides to get a breath of air and lands in the local pub. She sits down. The fellow sitting beside her says, 'Are you new around here?' Judy says, 'No, I've been in a relationship that's just ended and I'm feeling pretty terrible. I thought I'd come up here to try and feel better.' He says, 'My name is Ralph and I can't believe your bad luck. I'd be the worst person in the world to be talking to. I'm a relationship disaster. Why, the longest I've ever lasted in a relationship would be three months.'

A peculiar thing happens. Judy starts to perk up. She becomes cute and flirty. Ralph says, 'Hey, this seems to be doing you some good. How about dinner?' They have dinner, and the rest, as they say in the classics, is history. They've become an item.

You just happen to be Judy's best friend. So you say, 'Hey, I understand you've got a new man. What's he like?' And Judy will say, 'He's an architect, he loves dogs, he drives a Jag, he's sensitive, caring, affectionate and he sure can dance!' *That's what Judy is telling herself.*

When Ralph walks out the door three months later, no-one is more shocked than our gal Jude. Is Judy stupid? No. She has a major *survival issue*. And so do most of us.

A survival issue has three parts. 1. It's something that happens when we're *youngish*. 2. Which *feels terrible*. 3. Over which we have *no control*.

The reason it feels so bad is because what happened involved rejection, loss or physical pain. We were out of control because we were physically too small, not sufficiently worldly wise and not powerful enough to stop it. The event can be as dramatic as being physically abused or as benign as being made fun of in the playground. There's a feeling of, 'I'm not going to survive this', either in the literal sense or in a self-esteem sense.

How do you know if you have a survival issue? Because you would have made a survival decision. *When I grow up, I'm never going to let this happen to me again.* Now, here comes the tricky part.

We think we've made the decision because of the 'feeling terrible' part. We think we didn't survive the pain. Wrong! Look again. What you'll see is that you went into pain management. We bury the pain somewhere and get on with life. We carry it around in some bearable way. Some people's pain is readily accessible and others have buried theirs deeper. But in any case, we've got some pain, and we're surviving *with* it. Or else we got over the pain. We *survived* the pain.

So, if our survival decision isn't about pain, and if we've grown up, it isn't about being young, that leaves only one thing. It's about being *out of control*! If you ask people what are the most important things in the world they'll tell you good health, love, peace of mind, sex, money, children and happiness. Truly, the most important thing to people is to *be in control*. What we think is unsurvivable is the loss of control.

What we're saying is, 'When I grow up, I'm never going to let this happen to me again *out of my control.*' So, how can we be *in control* of being in pain? There's only one way. *Cause it!* I can hear rational minds screaming, 'Why would we *cause* something so painful?' I'm not saying this is rational. It's simply what we do.

Bryan's father was a career serviceman in the navy, and often away from home. Bryan's mother came to depend on him. He was her favourite and she referred to him as 'her little man'. Bryan loved his position of power in the household and over his two sisters.

One day, Bryan was meant to be going to sea scouts after school, but realised he'd left in the morning without his ropes manual. When he returned home to collect it, he surprised his mother in bed with their neighbour from across the street.

Bryan's sense of betrayal was enormous. He was inconsolable. The pain he felt made him despondent. He vowed he'd never be with a woman who would be unfaithful. When he became mutually besotted with his wife, Fiona, he simply overlooked the fact she was dating one of his classmates. Four years into their marriage, Bryan caught Fiona with a close friend in a back bedroom at a party. They both pleaded alcohol-induced diminished responsibility. A month later she announced she was leaving him for his friend.

Bryan was devastated but there was a little voice in the back of his head that said, 'I knew this was going to happen. This is what always happens.'

Let's go back to Judy. She picks her men by radar. When

she meets them, they give her that one little clue, 'I only hang around for three months,' 'I'm not sure I want a committed relationship,' 'I get bored easily,' 'No-one's going to trap me,' 'What do you mean, "do I love you", I'm *here* aren't I?' Every one of these messages is fraught with potential pain.

Also, typically, the rest of the man is charming, good-looking, intelligent and successful. The fact that he's not a stayer is neatly tucked into her subconscious, perhaps never to come up for air again. But it's his one characteristic that's of value to her. This combination is what lets Judy know this is her man.

Every time a man she loves walks out the door she is in agony, but there's a little voice inside that says, 'See! I knew that would happen! That's what always happens to me.' And, of course, it does, because Judy makes it happen either through selection or by behaving in a way that finally forces them to leave. Some of the things men have said to her include, 'I really love you, but your behaviour is unacceptable to me,' 'There's a wall half a metre thick around you,' 'You always make me out to be in the wrong,' 'I can never win with you.' Judy never sees her behaviour as being the catalyst for her relationships ending up on the scrap heap.

You see, if Judy picked a fair dinkum, honest-to-God contender for a real relationship, loved him, trusted him, was willing to be vulnerable with him and *then* he abandoned her, she would have a total re-enactment of her survival issue with her father. This would include being totally out of control. She believed he'd never leave her and without her *causing* it, he left.

What's the solution for Judy or anyone who has a survival issue? There's a way out. The antidote for a survival decision is to make a *new* decision. At the age of five, six, seven or any age where we experience something that causes significant pain and loss of control for the first time, we really do believe that we may not survive. It's not an inappropriate response, considering. Considering what? Considering we were young, inexperienced and impotent in the circumstances.

Once we have made the decision — that we wouldn't survive, that we'll never let this happen to us again, out of our control — we go on behaving in a way appropriate to that decision. We do this by picking wrong partners or sabotaging our relationships. We don't go back to the original experience and ask ourselves, 'Was my decision accurate?' It may have been true then but is it true *now*?

A fact: being rejected is never going to feel good. It's always going to be a ten on the Richter scale. Unless you've had an emotional by-pass, the normal response is always going to be pain, maybe even agony. But *it is survivable*. Being in agony is not the same thing as not surviving. People who think rejection is an impossibility are fools, but people who live life as though it were a probability are cowards.

If this is the game of life, we have two choices. Play or don't play. Not playing is safe, but you're not really living. The best it gets is to get through it. The toll for playing is that sometimes it doesn't feel good, but at least you know you're alive. The cure for a survival issue is to know that the price for choosing the *right* partner is the risk of agony and the willingness to play anyway.

Sometimes, moving forwards means we have to stop going backwards.

Tossing Out
the Old

I walk for an hour every morning. Except when I don't. When I don't, I make excuses for why I didn't. If it's good enough, I can buy into my excuse. 'It wasn't just a flu, it was a debilitating flu. It wasn't just jet lag, it was delayed flight-type jet lag.' That sort of thing. In this way I can justify not walking for a few more days.

Now, this behaviour isn't a capital offence, but it explains why New Year's resolutions rarely work. New Year's resolutions are almost always about what we promise ourselves we'll do in the new year. So if we look at the above confession, the logical commitment for me would be to promise to walk more next year. Wrong. What I'd be missing is the fact that my excuses actually contribute to my not walking. I need to resolve to stop making excuses.

As a psychologist, people come to me because they want to change something about themselves. Something about the way they are doing things isn't working. They want different results in their lives.

When my clients and I get to work on the jigsaw puzzle of

their lives, we examine origins, belief systems, patterns, significant events and decisions. Finally the whole picture is on the table and becomes clear to both of us.

What happens at this point, inevitably, is that my client will say, 'OK, I understand how I got to this point and why I am the way I am, but what do I *do* about it?' Here's what I have observed: the solution is rarely about what they should do, it's about what they should stop doing.

Kirsten's parents got divorced when she was four, but it wasn't particularly traumatic for her. Kirsten was a golden girl, pretty, bright, effervescent. Of three siblings, she was the favourite of both parents. Her father eventually remarried and Kirsten picked up another fan. Kirsten's Dad and step mother had a baby girl, Bianca. Kirsten adored her. Life was a series of win-win experiences.

This lasted until Kirsten was sixteen. Insurmountable problems developed between her Dad and step mother. Her step mother took Bianca and moved to the States. The wrench from her step sister was awful. This was her first loss of an important relationship.

Kirsten took on the role of the commiserating mate to her Dad, which brought them even closer. Two years later, the step mother announced she was sending Bianca back to Australia. Suddenly, Kirsten's Dad realised he had a chance to grasp a lost opportunity, to get close to the daughter he thought he'd lost. Kirsten was dethroned as favourite child. And there was worse to come. Kirsten's father was threatened by Kirsten's relationship with Bianca. He wanted Bianca exclusively so he rejected Kirsten. Second loss.

Kirsten's first love interest went overseas on a planned trip he was taking before settling down forever with Kirsten. She never heard from him again.

Kirsten is now in a relationship with a man she loves. Her self-described behaviour is 'erratic', 'over-demanding' and 'becoming intolerable to him'. She came to me because she could see the writing on the wall. She doesn't want to lose him but she can't stop her behaviour.

When the whole picture was put on the table, the situation became clear. Kirsten's suffering had been caused by the unexpected loss of close relationships, and there was no way she ever wanted to be out of control in another situation where she might be rejected. Her behaviour towards her boyfriend was an attempt to maintain control.

If he was going to reject her, it was going to be because of her unacceptable behaviour. Her gain in this scenario is that when it's over she doesn't have to agonise about being rejected because of something innately inadequate about herself. She can say it may have worked if only she hadn't behaved so abominably.

It's at this point that the inevitable question gets asked. 'OK. I see it. I understand why I'm doing it, but if I don't stop he's going to leave me. I don't want that to happen. What can I do?'

I ask her if she can afford to be in a relationship she doesn't sabotage. Can she handle it if she stops behaving badly, and a perfect partner does nothing wrong, but one day just decides that he doesn't love her any more. Will she survive?

She thinks about it. 'Yes. It would be hard, but I'd be OK. So how can I change?'

Stop being a pain in the neck. Give the guy a break. Take yourself out of the too-hard basket. If you find yourself slipping, ask yourself if you really have to do this. If you do, then apologise. Take responsiblity for yourself. If you can't stop yourself, explain to him what's going on. Reassure him he's not the cause of your behaviour. Tell him you're working on it but for the time being you can't help yourself and that he's free to ignore you. You'll tell him when it's over.

There was nothing for Kirsten to do as much as there was something she needed to stop doing. 'As easy as that?' she asked. It's not easy, because old habits die hard. But, yes, it's as simple as that.

Imagine you have a small child who's taken to hitting other children in the playground. Your child comes home in despair about the fact that the other children won't play with him. He has no friends. The solution isn't about what he should do, but what he should stop doing.

Landmark dates are significant. They're a good time for change. Birthdays and Mondays feel like resetting-the-clock days. And just the title 'New Year' suggests a fresh start. So it's a good opportunity for transformation. All I'm saying is that perhaps the focus shouldn't always be on what you promise to do, but what you promise not to do.

Feel the difference between saying, 'Next year I'm going to find the right relationship' and 'Next year I'm going to stop picking destructive partners.' The first has a feel of happening in the never-never. The second feels like it's quite specific and a lot less laden with effort.

In general, a truth about human transformation is that it

seems psychologically easier to think about stopping a behaviour than to take on a new behaviour. Often a change for the better has to do with a pattern that's a symptom, not a cause. If you overeat because you are angry at your mother, you can work on ways to stop being angry at your mother which in turn will cause you to lose weight. Or you can go on a diet. But the diet won't help you when you're angry. It's amazing how all right we'd be if we'd merely let go of our own self-inflicted wounds.

We need to take responsibility for our own behaviour in order to prevent ourselves becoming responsible for someone else's behaviour. An inappropriate behaviour to be on the lookout for is that of the love addict.

Please Paddle My Canoe

A re you in a relationship and feeling uneasy? Do you have a sense that if you were to even *think* about getting out, you'd be hung for treachery? Do you feel as though if you were to question your love, you'd break into a guilt sweat? Do you ever think that instead of a relationship, you've got an entanglement, an entrapment? If so, your partner may be a love addict.

In the eighties, the focus would have been on you. You would have been called a co-dependent. That was the term given to the partners of addicts, whether the addiction be to alcohol, drugs or gambling. You would have been diagnosed as having a saviour complex. But after the movie *Fatal Attraction* the floodlight switched to a new obsession. It's called love addiction.

The most common cause of love addiction is a sense of love deprivation as a child. The love-starved child develops a belief that, 'If my own parents don't love me, no-one ever will. I'm not good enough for anyone to love.' When they finally do form a love relationship, their feelings of being loved are exaggerated. It's what they've craved for years. The starvation turns into addiction.

The love recipient has their first experience of feeling adequate, valuable, worthy and appreciated. All these sensations are attributable to their partner. The partner is the source, the reason they feel so wonderful. They hand over the entire responsibility for their well-being to their partner. This relationship is doomed.

At first the partner will be flattered at having such a powerful effect on someone. Eventually they begin to resent the onus of burden for such a heavy weight of responsibility. They're no longer hearing 'I love you'. They're hearing 'I need you'. The dependency becomes unbearable. As the addict begins to feel the partner pull away, their insecurity and need can turn to panic. They feel, 'I can't make it without my partner.' The partner has no permission to get out.

The second cause of love addiction is an experience of an earlier relationship rejection. The sufferer has such a terrible memory of the anguish they endured, they feel that if it were to happen again they wouldn't pull through.

Almost simultaneously with realising how much they love their partner, they get in touch with how terrible it would be if they were to lose their love object. This shows up as moodiness, inordinate jealousy and tyrannical behaviour in an attempt to gain control over their partner. It's a manipulation aimed at making the partner feel guilty, inadequate at pleasing them or scared. Anything as long as it keeps them in the relationship.

No matter how much the partner tries to please and allay the addict's fears, it's to no avail. It's never enough. The addict might believe that their insecurity arises from a lack of sufficient dedication from the partner. Some fail to see that their own tyrannical behaviour is what is causing the gulf. Others are aware of what they are doing but can't stop themselves. Even if the partner is willing to subjugate their needs to the addict totally, there's no surer outcome for this relationship than disaster. It's a time bomb.

The third cause of love addiction comes from a disorder I call 'only child-itis'. You don't have to be an only child to have the disorder. You can also get it from being the favourite. This is the way it happens. The first time you open your eyes as a baby, you see peering down at you four adoring eyes looking as though they were witnessing a miracle. The way this makes you feel is adorable. What happens is you *become* adorable. The more adorable you become, the more adoring the audience becomes, which in turn causes you to escalate the adorableness, and on it goes. People with only child-itis are incredibly charismatic, and pretty near irresistible.

Sufferers of o.c. are often centre stage, have a million friends and are life's winners. They usually get a golden run at life and lead a charmed existence. That is, until they receive their first significant rejection. This usually arrives later than the kick in life's teeth the rest of us mere mortals received years earlier because we weren't all that adorable. Two things happen to these people. First, they go into deep shock. Second, they are inconsolably shattered. Their minds scream, 'How could this possibly have happened? Didn't he/she know it was *me*? This happens to other people. It doesn't happen to *me*!'

Rejection is terrible for all of us, but just picture what it would be like if you'd gone through life as a constant winner. Why wouldn't you think it would go on forever? It isn't as though you took it for granted, it's just that you wouldn't have ever known anything else. When a drop-kicked o.c. sufferer shows up in my office, I know I'm in for a full tissue box session.

It's what happens between shocked and shattered that's the worry. Only child-itis victims can take an inordinately long time to accept that the rejection is an actuality. Don't forget they've had an experience completely out of their range of reality. Their behaviour can look pretty obsessive. 'If I just try this, or this, or this, they'll realise the irresistibility that's me.'

The prognosis for love addicts who are afflicted with only child-itis is good. It will take them longer to recover from the relationship break-up than it does ordinary folk, but once they're at the end of the nightmare, they get back their adorableness, with an added dimension of sensitivity, empathy and more understanding of others. Now they're not just adorable, they're true co-partner material.

What kind of people are the guilt-ridden, long-suffering, trapped partners? 'Nice' people. The problem they have is bumping into their own self-concept, the picture they have about who they see themselves as being. 'How can I possibly think of my own needs, when my partner is so impoverished? How can I be so insensitive, so callous, so selfish?'

What the partner needs to decide is whether they're going to donate their lives to a charitable organisation — the addict. Or whether they are willing to cash in their 'nice guy' card and do something very difficult, which is to tell the truth to the addict, and then get their own needs met? 'I really love you, but this relationship doesn't work.' Or, 'As much as I love you, I'm having enough trouble paddling my own canoe. I just don't have the energy to paddle yours too.' This may not be easy, but at least it's honest.

In working with the addict, they will swear that everything they do for their partner is done because of how much they love them. Keep in mind, they will do *anything* they think will keep the partner in the relationship, often at their own expense and self-sacrifice. It's not until the following questions get asked that reality starts to enter the picture.

I ask them, 'If you love your partner that much, you'd want them to be happy. Is that right?

'Yes, that's right.'

'What if freedom is what would make your partner really happy? What if ending the relationship with you would make them really happy? Do you love them that much, that their happiness could be more important to you than your own?'

Now the real work begins. Love addicts are often shocked at the discovery that the passion of their emotion has nothing to do with love or their partner. It has to do with dependency, insecurity and need. In fact, any partner who could remedy those inadequacies would suffice. The partner is not a 'who' but a 'what'. They're not a person, they're a solution.

The love addict must develop an awareness that it's not love to which they're addicted. For the love-deprived, it's about finding a solution to their emptiness. For the tyrant, it's the best way to avoid being rejected. For the only child-itis sufferer it's the need to be right about their concept of themselves.

The cure? Re-education. The addict has to see that the

source of their well-being must come from within themselves in order for them to ever feel secure. Other people's love can come and go. Partners can end relationships, they can die. The experience of *self*-worth, *self*-esteem and *self*-love can never be taken away. If there is no-one else there for you, you can be there for yourself.

The prognosis? Good, if the addict is willing to admit there's a problem and is willing to seek help. More often than not, the result of therapy is that they start to generate a different look. They begin to appear independent, self-contained, confident, worthy of respect, at peace within themselves.

I often call therapy 'the process of learning to stand up inside yourself'. I mean this psychologically, emotionally and even physically. The reasons a person can end up a deflated shell are numerous. Every new-born baby has confidence and self-esteem, a sense of themselves as the embodiment of perfection. If you walked up to a baby's crib and said, 'Hey, dummy, ugly, clumsy, stupid', they'd continue looking at you with a silly smile and absolutely no loss of positive self-perception.

It isn't until a child hears those disparaging remarks, makes the connection they are aimed at them and then makes the fatal mistake of taking those criticisms personally, that they exit the emotional Garden of Eden. The child is now battling self-doubt, shame and lack of belief in themself. Whatever heights of well-being within themself they had achieved up to now are eroded. Their self-esteem can end up at ground zero.

It is with this flattened sense of self that a person may find that therapy can help lift their confidence, self-opinion and ability to get their needs met, and make them a better candidate for meeting someone else's needs, thereby making them better relationship material.

As therapy continues this person can start to see themself in a different light. They gain a perspective of the events of the past, seeing things with a different perception, with new-found skills to handle what they could not handle previously because of lack of age, wisdom and strength.

The addict is now able to stand up inside themself. Ultimately, the love addict becomes capable of letting go of the partner. The partner now has a real *choice* about whether or not to be in the relationship. It's amazing how often just the permission to choose whether or not to get out creates the freedom for the partner to choose to stay in.

Now that you're paddling your own canoe, how about paddling one with someone else?

Learning to Paddle Together

Margaret's complaint: 'Andrew isn't affectionate or intimate any more. I'm worried we're growing apart.'

Andrew's response: 'She's right, I feel the distance as well. She puts me down a lot, I feel like I'm always being judged. It sort of puts a damper on my feelings.'

Margaret's response: 'What am I supposed to do? Make him feel like he's God's gift to the female gender? I hate women who play that game. Why should we have to? I don't like women who feel they have to suck up to and flirt with men.'

My response to Margaret's response: 'Margaret, you can't have it both ways. You're acting like you don't like him, and then wondering why he doesn't feel warm towards you. Why are you with him? Why are you here trying to fix things up?'

Margaret: 'Are you suggesting that I tell him the things I like about him, *out loud*?'

OK. That's it! No more Mrs Nice Shrink! My gloves are off. I'm fighting mad.

Over fifty per cent of my practice is male. From where I'm sitting, they're lost. Hopelessly and utterly adrift. And their female partners seem intent on tossing them ballast instead of life jackets — even if the cost is that they both sink.

I'm not anti-female. Women soothe my soul. I'd rather do a spell at a philatelic convention than suffer the boredom of lunch with the boys. I'd cancel anything to lunch with the girls.

Look at the Humpty Dumpty rhyme. The king is certainly liable for a work discrimination suit (if not a negligence claim), by calling on all of his *men* to put Humpty back together again.

Women tend to be better at healing, nurturing and succour.

But Humpty Dumpty is a good analogy for men. When women got angry, we pushed hard and a lot of men toppled. Since their descent, women have failed to notice that something peculiar has happened to us as well. When men fell off the wall, we got to see that, just like us, they're as breakable as eggshells.

Are women angry at men for manipulating them through false advertising? Are we seizing the moment and going for the jugular like one would a cornered animal we see as having supremacy over us? Or are women frustrated because men aren't what they seemed, and we liked the fantasy of them seated above us, icon-like on the wall, the egg in shining armour? Something about them appearing 'mere' has done something funny to all of us.

When men misbehave in relationships, their tactic is to bully, either physically, financially or verbally. But they've been sprung. Volumes have been written on the matter. Our SWAT team is onto them. And so it should be.

But maybe, just maybe, it's time we blew the whistle on

ourselves. The truth is that some women, when it comes to men, are covert, judgmental and play dirty. I know. I really like men and I've done it.

I think it all started when women discovered men had the brawn and we didn't. If they thoroughly cheesed us off, we didn't have thumping them as an option. So women put on their thinking caps and came up with a ploy that makes ASIO operatives look like they belong in the sandbox!

Women know how to make men *feel disgusting about themselves*. This truly is our most powerful weapon.

True confession time. Ask yourself if you're guilty of any of the following:

1.   It's your wedding anniversary (insert meaningful occasion). You've received nothing, not even a card (insert meaningful token). He comes home for dinner. You assume he'll compensate. It hasn't occurred to him. The resentment mounts. You go quiet. He eventually says, 'What's the matter?' And you say, 'If you don't know, *then don't worry about it!!!*' Result: he feels disgusting about himself (sometimes without even knowing why, but he's supposed to know if he really understands us, without us even having to tell him).

2.   He's too long at the pub. He's a jerk at the party. He ogles a babe at the beach. He wimps out of the birthing classes. How long does it take before we start projecting feelings of '*If you really loved me,* you would never have done that.' Result: he feels disgusting about himself.

3.   You and your partner are invited to a friend's home for dinner. The guest of honour is Arnold, a notable war correspondent, visiting from New York. He's just back from Rwanda

and recounting how many orphans he was able to single-handedly save. Your partner left the table ten minutes ago, to go to the loo, you thought. You excuse yourself and find him in the lounge room, door closed, volume turned down. He's watching a State of Origin game. Your pronouncement: 'What kind of a meat-head could be more interested in football than a first-hand report about what's going on in the world?' Result: he feels disgusting about himself.

If women don't *need* men, we have to make up our minds whether our lives are better with them in it or not. If women don't like men, if we're not prepared to let them make it with us, that's OK, but then we should have the integrity to be honest about it. If we decide to include them, do we really need to be so mean of spirit, to deny them the acknowledgment of the value of their contribution? Are we too mean to be gracious *out loud*?

Are women walking on such thin ice that if we let men be right every so often we'd lose our power, our autonomy, our identities? Is our victory so shallow that we'd lose our edge if we let go of our high moral ground?

Back to the Humpty Dumpty predicament. A lot of men are in pieces, teetering on the eggshell of political correctness, not knowing who to be around us, not knowing how on earth to get back into our good books.

The stand-off we're at is contributed to by women's resentment, our withholding of any positive feedback, as though if we didn't hold back, we'd be selling out to the enemy. If women want to get it fixed, we're the ones who can do it. We've won. We've got to move on from being 'right'. If it were Humpty in strife, we'd assist. It's not. It's men.

Men should ask women, 'Why does wanting to look after you have to be translated into looking down on you? What's so awful about wanting to tuck you under my wing? I didn't say shoe. What terrible thing would happen to you, if you let me feel pleased with myself over something I've done for you?'

Here's a challenge to men. When your partner brings up an issue, listen very carefully to the content and take heed. Take her seriously. Let her know you understand what she's communicated. *But* don't be manipulated by judgment messages. If you start to detect that 'What kind of a person' tone of voice, get ready. Here comes one.

Keep in mind that your needs are as important and valid as hers. Your responsibility to yourself is to press on regardless. Have the courage to be fair but set limits, women know when their manipulation bluff is called. We respect you as a man all the more for it.

I think we've stated our case. We've raised consciousness. Men know we have a point. The more enlightened ones know they need to do and think things differently. We need to do what comes next: support, motivate, encourage and positively reinforce.

SEX &
Sensuality

No relationship book would be complete without touching on the potential minefield of sex. Sex isn't everything in a relationship, but it's a good thermometer to gauge the temperature of the relationship. If relationships are where love gets played, then sex is the part where the lie detector gets played. More lies of omission are told in bed than anywhere else.

We need to say it the way it is for us, let the chips fall where they may and hope that love and commitment will take a guiding hand to steer us along the path of communication, compromise and solution. Long-term sex doesn't need to be the best either has ever had, but it has to work. Things between ourselves and others rarely work if they're not communicated about. Intimacy and sensuality are just as important as sex.

✴

Sleeping With Friends

T here's an old saying, 'If you lie down with a friend, you may wake up with an enemy.' Well, there should be.

Raise your hand if you haven't got an example of a relationship where you stepped too far over the wrong line. You'd be in the minority. Almost all of us have at least one example where we wish we could roll back the clock so a relationship could go back to where it appropriately belonged.

There seem to be four case scenarios for friendship becoming sexual. The first is where both parties have always had some sexual spark and have had to douse it because there was a taboo on the relationship. Perhaps one or both parties had an involvement with a family member or close friend. For instance, your sister is married to a man that you are sexually attracted to. You feel the same attraction from him. Or your best mate has a girlfriend you fancy, and you sense that in different circumstances the feeling would be reciprocated. In these instances settling for friendship is what is called for.

If the other party's relationship with the family member or friend terminates, then the friendship status of the sexually attracted parties can change. It's a good idea to allow a respectable amount of time to pass before this new liaison becomes public. In this way, the family or friend doesn't misread that the breakdown of their relationship was caused by this outside factor.

It's important to make sure that the sexual attraction isn't caused by the excitement of the clandestine and taboo nature of the expression of your feelings. There needs to be more substance to your feelings than simply sexual magnetism. If this is not investigated, then the sexual fantasy of forbidden fruit may get played out and then the reason for the relationship becomes redundant. If taken slowly and carefully, this is an example where a friendship which becomes sexual can work.

Then there's the variation of the *When Harry Met Sally* plot. During a long friendship one party has always been sexually attracted to the other but the feelings weren't reciprocated. Or neither party has felt any sexual affinity, but through the course of the friendship an emotional and psychological intimacy has evolved. The progression of this intimacy can result in a mutual desire for sexual intimacy. Much of the groundwork for a relationship with a deep foundation has been laid before it was sexually consummated. Not only can this change of status of a relationship work, but it should work well.

Those are the happy ending examples. More commonly what turns out to need damage control are the following scenarios. Two opposite sex members develop a friendship. Neither party is sexually interested in the other. Time together, mutual experiences and shared feelings happen. There's a real sense of caring and closeness, and genuine feelings of love.

What the principals experience is that the relationship has reached a ceiling. They sense their union should be moved along to some further place, that there's a dimension left unexplored that should be explored. The feelings of love can be confusing. This can be true especially if one or the other has never had a close relationship with the opposite sex on a platonic level. So they cross the physical boundary.

If there weren't honest sexual stirrings on each part, but curiosity or a sense that they should progress the relationship's status, they are in for trouble. Now confusion, discomfort and awkwardness are the order of the day. There's a sense of, 'Oh, oh. What do we do now? This feels all wrong.'

The other disaster is where one friend has always secretly fancied the other friend but keeps it under wraps. One day the pressure gets too much or the timing seems conducive. The attracted partner makes a move and puts the hard word on the disinterested party. The disinterested friend can comply out of guilt for denying the need of such a close person. Or out of an idealised feeling that if it could work, it would be perfect because everything else is in place.

My feeling is that the phenomenon called animal attraction or sexual chemistry is real. When boy meets girl something either happens or it doesn't. The trouble is, there is no rational reason why there is or isn't that spark.

You know that perfect date, the one where the person meets every criterion known to man or woman, where their résumé reads like a *Who's Who* entry? This is the one where your parents and friends all sit around with their fingers crossed, hoping. And you walk in the door afterwards with disappointment written all over your face.

As I've said before, if you're hot, you're hot. If you're not, you're not. If your feelings weren't sexual in the first place, there is a reason. The most likely one is that for one or both persons there was no sexual chemistry. That the relationship became friendship instead of romance most probably describes the honest expression of how it really should be.

Well, we all make mistakes. What do you do if you've gone too far? First of all, it's embarrassing. It doesn't get more personal than being emotionally and physically exposed and sexually involved. You've gone and done it with someone who feels like your brother or sister and there's no undoing it. You have to accept that.

Now there's talking about it. How do you tell someone that you really care about, and that you'd really like to keep in your life, that you don't want to have sex with them ever again? How can you do this and not hurt their feelings?

Persevere at all costs. Lovers come and go. Sexual attraction is inexpensive, common and effortless. Chemistry just is. Friendship is precious, takes time to develop, requires maintenance and care, and is an investment.

Say it the way it is. If it's true friendship then it shouldn't be conditional. It should be based on honesty. 'I really love you and would do anything I could for you, but a sexual relationship with you doesn't reflect the truth about my feelings for you.'

The friendship may have to take some time out. The sexually spurned friend may have to handle their feelings of rejection. And the friend who inappropriately accommodated the sexual invitation may have to get over some feelings of guilt and awkwardness. But as soon as one feels like they are ready to resume the friendship, they should contact the other to see how they are doing. If the other isn't ready, respect that. But make it clear that you'll be waiting and ready as soon as they are.

Friendship calls for selflessness and a commitment to the other's well-being. It also calls for personal integrity, sincerity and truthfulness. It should be big enough to withstand an honest mistake.

Whatever you do, if you want a friend to be more than a friend, don't ...

Kiss and Tell

There's a saying in my game, 'Be careful what you wish for, because you may get it.' I had a forty-year-old male client, married twelve years, with two children, nine and five. His complaint: not enough sex. The solution: leave wife and move in with a much younger woman. Sex? Plethora! 'She offers oral sex while I'm driving, which my wife would have considered a moving violation!' State of mind? 'Bliss!' For a while.

My question: 'What's wrong?' Answer: 'I feel pressured. Not only does she want sex morning, noon and night, but because I know she's had a million guys before me, I'm self-conscious. She's actually berated me about my performance on occasion, when I've been really tired. Not only am I beginning to dread going to bed, but I'm missing my wife. I think that I actually prefer her sexuality. Sure, I didn't get it as often as I wanted, but I miss the mystery of it. There was something exciting about the chase, of not knowing if I would or wouldn't score, and the sweet sense of victory when I did.'

Another saying, 'The more things change, the more they stay the same.' For centuries, deeply ingrained in the male psyche has been the concept or reality of 'man the hunter'. Lately, we've been indoctrinated with the propaganda that hunting is now a gender-free activity. A deluge of magazine articles has told us how we women can make up for lost time and get our own back: 'Ten steps towards creative infidelity,' 'How to politically outmanoeuvre in a male-dominated office,' etc. In other words, let's take what men do to us that we find sleazy or hateful and do it better to them.

Is that what Andie MacDowell is doing in the cafe scene in *Four Weddings and a Funeral?* Not exactly. In answer to Hugh Grant's question about how many lovers she's had, she answers with the ease of putting a knife through room temperature butter on a hot summer's day. Not only was the answer thirty-three, but they were listed in chronological order with anecdotal information. I personally couldn't answer the same question with as much fluency if it pertained to the number of chocolate chip ice-creams I've enjoyed. And I'm pretty passionate about chocolate chip ice-cream.

Am I casting moral aspersions here? No, not at all. Is it wrong for a female to participate in thirty-three affairs? No it's not. Is it wrong to tell a prospective lover you've had thirty-three affairs? No, it's not wrong; but there's a gamble that it won't work. After years of balancing being a female, whose gender is in revolt, while at the same time consulting with men in relationship, what becomes ever more clear is the paradox between what's fair and what works.

What's at risk is this. If a man has had thirty-three affairs, many women would find that attractive. It would augur well on the experience proficiency scoreboard. It's widely believed that most men are predominantly sexual versus emotional. So it's perfectly conceivable that a man may have had sex with thirty-three women but felt nothing for any of them. We can remain hopeful that we'll be the one to walk off with the totality trophy.

On the other hand, it's widely believed that women are predominantly emotional versus sexual. So if she had thirty-three lovers it's a possibility she felt something for most of them.

Many women would confess that at least once they've been the victim of a man's sexual objectification and then been dumped ('He only wanted me for one thing'). Most bounce back and survive.

It is my experience that men do not give their hearts away as readily as their sperm. Sometimes it only takes one major catastrophe in judging with whom to trust his heart to have him end up in the damaged goods department, if not forever, for a long time.

Seventy-five per cent of married men admit to extracurricular sex, while only forty per cent of women admit to having done likewise. However, the rate of divorce attributed to female infidelity is significantly greater than that of divorce attributed to male infidelity. What this suggests is that marriage seems able to withstand male digression because the institution is threatened predominantly by physical jeopardy, whereas there appears to be far greater jeopardy caused by a female's emotional and psychological involvement with someone else.

This also helps to explain the goose and gander quandary. On an instinctual level, men intuit that women are more 'involved' when it comes to sex, therefore their betrayal is seen to be on a deeper, broader and more perilous level. Men can randomly stray and return. Women tend to focus and leave, either because of the depth of feeling for the other man or because of dissatisfactory contrasts to her current partner that the new partner highlights. Men can be sexually numerous on an 'and' basis. Women who have a greater proclivity towards monogamy are more prone to be involved on an 'or' basis. Even Andie inferred her affairs were in tandem, not concurrent.

Look, if it were a perfect world, sex would be about making love as a form of shared intimacy and discovery. The risk in Andie MacDowell's divulgence is that it could make a person feel like sex as competition. Like having your date ask you to go dancing and finding yourself in the audition scene of *A Chorus Line*. It could make a person want to grab their dancing shoes and exit stage left. Being allowed to kiss and tell is fair, but unfortunately it runs the risk of not working.

When you've decided on 'the one', the game changes.

Is There Life After Infidelity?

B oy meets girl. Girl meets boy. They fall in love. They marry. They have children. Time passes. Husband has affair. Husband leaves wife. Wife is devastated. Time passes. Husband wants to return to wife. What are the chances for this relationship? Is there life after infidelity?

There is but it's hard. Very, very hard. Here's why.

Maggie and Bill enter my office. He looks like he's been sprung skywriting 'There's No Santa Claus' above Disneyland. She looks like she got caught kissing a steamroller. They've been through a bit.

I ask them what they want. Maggie starts to cry. Bill winces.

Maggie says, 'You're the one who made this appointment. You tell her.'

Bill says, 'Look I've made a stupid mistake. I've hurt my wife a hell of a lot, but I still love her and I'd like to make our marriage work.'

'And what would you like, Maggie?'

'I still love him but I'm not sure I can ever trust him again.'

The first step for this relationship is to acknowledge that

it's over. The relationship they had when they walked in the door didn't work. It's riddled with the dry rot of treachery, pain and guilt. Now it's important to officially end their relationship. This provides a choice as to whether to rechoose a partnership with each other or not, and creates a clean slate on which to work. It suggests the optimism of a fresh start, a new beginning, and eliminates the likelihood of carrying pollution from the past into the future.

The cause of this relationship not working was Bill, who has a flaw that was fatal: he wasn't committed. Maggie may or may not have a relationship flaw. If she does, Bill is far too guilty to bring it up now. We won't get to work on that one for a while.

The next step separates the men from the boys. Bill is going to have to make himself available for Maggie's story. Maggie has had an emotionally life-threatening experience. She's been betrayed, rejected and humiliated. She suffers the stigma of the female version of being a cuckold, 'not able to hold her man'.

Her self-esteem is somewhere around her ankles. Her sense of herself as a woman is diminished. She's in pain. What all this leads to- is that she is going to need healing. The most effective form of treatment is catharsis: the more she gets out, the less she has in. She needs to talk about it, and talk about it, and talk about it. She also needs to know that she's being received and understood.

Maggie has been hit by an emotional truck and she needs to communicate about it. Bill, who wants to be her partner, is the one with whom she needs to communicate. She needs to know that he empathises with her experience. It's terrible seeing someone he loves in so much pain. It was Bill driving the truck.

Bill is about to have the most profound experience of being wrong he's ever had. Every instinct he has to duck and defend has to be counteracted. He has to focus his intention on having her believe that he truly understands what has happened to her. Bill is going to want to say, 'That was all in the past. Can't we forget about it? She doesn't mean anything to me any more. Do we really have to go over this again? I'm here aren't I?'

The energy level of his apology is the weathervane for reading his sincerity. It has to match the energy level of her pain: 'I'm sorry. I'm so sorry.' He needs to be willing to allow Maggie's need to express herself to be more important than his need to defend his ego.

This is not a punishment. It is the first step towards intimacy and commitment. It won't work if he can't get past this step. She'll become a broken record until she feels she's had her communication understood. Not fixed, just understood.

Now Bill and I have some heavy-duty work to do on monogamy and commitment. He's battle-worn from the trauma of all this upheaval. The usual response is, 'Do you really think, in my right mind, I'd do this again? Look at the drama it's caused!'

That's not good enough. Bill has to choose monogamy for himself, not because of the strife it's got him into. At the least he needs to know that he'd never do it again because he would never want to hurt Maggie again. I remind him that monogamy isn't about never wanting to have a relationship with another woman again. It's about wanting to and knowing that you can turn it down anyway. Otherwise it's not a sufficiently binding commitment to keep him out of harm's way if the temptation were strong enough again. Bill needs to be able to trust *himself* before he can ask Maggie to trust him.

I had a client who left his wife for another woman. He told me until then he had been the most committed man he'd known. If he were seated next to an attractive woman on a business flight he'd ask to have his seat changed. When he reached his destination, he'd call his wife late at night and speak lovingly to her to prove there couldn't have been another woman in his bed. Which of them was he trying to convince? I'm protective. I wouldn't advise Maggie to get back into the lion's den until both Bill and I are convinced he's a trustworthy lion.

They've agreed to end their previous relationship with each other and start anew. Bill has been able to be acutely wrong. He's achieved successful empathic listening. Maggie is convinced that he understands what she has been through. Bill has graduated from monogamy school. The final hurdle about life after infidelity remains with Maggie.

At a certain point, it becomes time to move on. The question is, can Maggie accept that Bill has hurt her as much as he has? The breach of trust involves memory that will not disappear quickly or easily. Can she turn his infidelity into a thread she weaves into the tapestry of their new relationship? Or will she always see the infidelity thread as the entire tapestry? This is my husband who once cheated on me, or this is the cheat who is my husband?

Before she answers this question, Maggie has to be

reminded this is not a simple feat. There's no such thing as a memory by-pass. There will be details associated with his affair: songs, restaurants, times of the year, snatches of phrases, that will sneak up and cause her pain, rage and humiliation.

Once she says she can accept his infidelity, she has to be responsible for her bad times. Maggie is going to feel upset and she's going to have to handle it. She can no longer put her feelings onto Bill. If she continues to make him feel wrong or bad about himself, he's going to feel defeated, as though he can never win. This can act as a cancer and undermine any possibility for a future together. If she can't accept his betrayal, she's better off admitting it and for them to go their separate ways.

When it comes to women being unfaithful, the psychology is different. As I have stated, statistically, when women have affairs, there is usually more involved than sex. The degree of intimacy involved in her affair will determine the length of time required for her to process her feelings.

Once a husband decides to renew his commitment to his marital partner, although he may still have some lingering feelings for the person with whom he had the affair, men aren't generally affected so much by those feelings. They are usually able to refocus on restoring their marriage more quickly.

One of the reasons for this is that men often stray because of the 'more is better' principal, but a woman more often has an affair because of something lacking in her marriage. When this is the case it is important that she be honest about whether the problem can be fixed sufficiently enough to trust herself to recommit.

When a wife has been unfaithful, it is imperative her husband be motivated to keep the marriage intact in order to be able to handle any ego problems he may have. Where men have the advantage is they are able to chop their feelings off. I don't mean bury them, I mean not have them any more. I've seen men return home from blazingly passionate, 'love of my life' affairs and hardly think another thought about the woman with whom they've been involved. Once the man decides he wants his marriage to work he can turn his energy back into loving his wife. I've also seen husbands devastated by a wife's affair have her return home and never look back.

Even after deciding she definitely wants to return to her marriage, women have a harder time with this. They are more affected behaviourally as well as emotionally by their feelings. They may remain in 'outer space', limbo, with a foot in both camps and have fits of depression for a period. This period takes patience for both of the rejected partners, but it often takes longer for the female partner to get through it.

If the spurned male partner will wait it out and doesn't have unrealistic expectations about the speed of her returned affection, passion and intimacy, he may well win in the end. Her appreciation for his understanding should pay off.

The good news is that once reunited, men in general are better tapestry weavers. They find it easier to put what has happened firmly in the past and move forward.

Infidelity can be crippling. To be crippled involves shock, pain and loss of confidence. Although debilitating, being crippled isn't fatal. With careful attention, patience and good intentions people have overcome all kinds of handicaps.

Throw in love, time and forgiveness and the outcome is equally optimistic.

The client who changed plane seats? He's back with his wife. He no longer has to wait till nightfall in a foreign place to speak lovingly to her. He relishes beautiful women. He feels free to sit next to them now. His wife? She doesn't mind. She trusts him.

It Was Just Sex

Please bear with me. I have bold-facedly generalised. There will be times when you'll say, 'But I know women who are like that,' or vice versa. I know. Trust me. I'll deal with the shoe being on the other foot later. This piece is statistically gender-biased.

Husband: 'She was *just* my secretary, for Pete's sake. Circumstances threw us together. There was nothing in it. It was *just sex*!!!'

Wife: sits quietly weeping, searching her tortured handkerchief for an unused space.

Thus begins the umpteenth case of marriage/relationship crisis that has begun exactly the same way over all my years in practice.

Ladies and gentlemen, spouses and partners, the bad news is that I've come to believe that 'male monogamy' is a contradiction in terms. I'm not saying there aren't monogamous men. I'm saying I've become convinced that monogamy for some men, like most males in the animal kingdom, is actually *unnatural*. It gets worse. I even suspect there's a scam attached to this issue.

The concept of male monogamy has the subtle scent of being a female-conceived plot, at best based on ignorance of the opposite sex; the naivety of thinking they're sexually wired like us. At worst, it's based on morality, self-righteousness and a desperate attempt at fidelity and 'keeping our men'. If we can make them feel bad enough about themselves we may be able to keep them on the straight and narrow.

Let's get real about male sexuality: A. They're horny. B. They're curious.

About being horny. There's that old chestnut about the physiological build-up of semen and sperm that creates mounting pressure and discomfort and needs to be relieved. But what about seventy-year-olds who aren't all that pressured any more who are still mighty sexy? I think it's the nature of the beast. Men are horny.

About being curious. It has been explained to me that the greatest fascination men have for women is that no two are alike. Every woman's sexual response is different. All their body parts are different. What turns one on, turns another off. What would work with this woman? How would she respond? Would I succeed? A virtual smorgasbord of potential delight. It would be easy here to infer that I'm accusing men of outrageous egotism. I'm not. I believe that it's geniune fascination. I have a brother. When I was playing with dolls, he was dismantling them to see how they worked.

About female sexuality:

A woman wants to be *real*ised, made to feel as though who she *is* is real to the man. This need to be *real*ised is not a concept or a romantic idealisation. It is an honest-to-God experience. Maybe it's because she perceives herself as the more vulnerable partner because she's the recipient, the one being literally entered, penetrated. She wants to believe that it's the internal essence of her being that he's attracted to. Women want their whole person made love to, not just their bodies.

A woman's sexuality is a lot about intimacy. It's a physical way of expressing 'I love or care about you'. Because of how she feels for him, she wants to give him her*self*, share her*self* with him. In the feelings package often included are trust, affection and closeness, and an expectation of being seen as special. Where she goes wrong is to make the assumption that he has come to the party with the same package of offerings and expectations. What men who are successful at 'scoring' know is: if you don't get into their heads, there's a chance you may not get into their pants.

Given this simplistic thumbnail sketch of our differences, it's a miracle that we get it together at all! And just to make matters worse, men are often hornier than women. In couples with disparate sexual appetites the numbers are two to one. Men want sex more often than women. Maybe this is because his sex drive is of a simpler, automatic, physiological nature. And hers, the drive to create a relationship and feel valued for her inner self.

Here's another thing. Many men have told me they can handle extra-marital/relationship sex. They say they can have sex with other women because they don't get enough at home (the horny factor) or (this one stings), sex with their primary partner is plentiful, fabulous, satisfying, 'the best I've ever had', but there's all this availability out there (the curiosity factor).

For whichever reason, unfaithful men swear they can do this and not have it negatively impact on their primary relationship (unless he gets sprung or a genitally transmitted disease). 'What about disloyalty and lies?' I ask. 'Why should I tell her something that means nothing and will only upset her?' they reply. I must confess in the past I have put these men into the category of lacking in feeling, unenlightened, stupid or liars.

I apologise. They can't all be lying. Furthermore, I can't tell you how many times I've had wives/girlfriends, victims of infidelity, tell me that they thought they had the happiest marriage/relationship in Australia *until they found out*. This backs up the theory that it's possible for infidelity not to negatively impact on the primary relationship.

So, does infidelity work? The answer is, unequivocally, *no*. And the reason is that although I really do believe that some guys can handle it, it simply *does not work for most women*. What this calls for is compromise, and it can't be from her. I didn't say she '*won't*' (she's not being stubborn), I'm saying most '*can't*'. I'm not calling this fair.

Remember, she's the one with sexuality related to soul mateship and her inner self. Her questions about infidelity are as rarely about performance as they are about, 'What did you talk about?' 'Did you hold her afterwards like you do me?' 'Does she make you laugh?' She'll find it incomprehensible that prettier, not prettier, bigger, smaller doesn't matter. Only that she was *different*. Her pain at the betrayal is enormous. Recuperation and restoration of trust is a long and arduous process, sometimes taking years. For some women, it's impossible and the relationship is doomed.

(There is a very small exception to the above rule which pertains to women whose libido is so low or whose sexual attraction to their partner is so non-existent that to have him seek sex elsewhere actually alleviates her guilt about sexually denying him. This is not mainstream.)

Also, I've generalised. There is plenty of cross-gender sexuality where what I've described as male pertains to female, and vice versa.

OK. What's the answer to this seemingly uncrossable chasm between the sexes?

1. We start saying it the way it is, instead of hanging onto some idealised notion of how it should be. For a lot of men, monogamy is not fundamentally or naturally the truth about the way they are.

2. It does not work for women for their men to be unfaithful.

3. The male is predominantly the one stuck with the compromise. Not an easy one. It can involve denying basic instinctive drives. He may be sexually craving and be willing to go hungry. He has to be willing to survive the 'wannas', as in he may wanna go to bed with his fitness trainer.

Why would any man in his right mind be willing to do something that involves denial and discomfort when it's not even for himself? And he won't even be thanked for it. There's only one reason. It's got to be for *her*. It has to be that she's so precious to him, she's worth it.

He needs to be mature enough to know that he's had enough experience out there in the field to know he's not going to feel ripped off or short-changed later on. He needs to be sure about what he's signing on for. If he makes this kind of commitment, he needs to be able to trust himself to be able to keep his word.

Statistically, the man I'm describing is rare. In my opinion? Worth the hunt, a treasure to find. Special.

Now that we've got that straightened out, how about some fine-tuning?

Are You a
Good Lover?

As we grow from babyhood to adulthood, and if we're fortunate, there seem to be three distinct aspects and stages of pleasure that constitute human sensuality.

Phase one of sensuality is *affection*. For many of us, this happens from birth in the form of physical sensations that we receive from our parents. The cooing, cuddling, hugs and kisses that take place when we're children give us our introduction to the tactile world of being close. We feel cared for bodily as well as psychologically. We experience wonderful physical sensations which make us feel nurtured and safe, close to others and secure.

The second phase starts as we become socialised creatures and venture out of home into the world of our peers. For most of us that means school, sport and play groups. Usually we find kindred spirits out there and develop friendships with soulmates who we feel are participating in our experiences on our level, people who have things we would like to share, such as toys, games, classroom events, gossip and secrets.

It feels more appropriate to be sharing these things with

our friends than our parents, because our friends are present in a reality that our parents aren't a part of any more. Our friends are our own age, at the same stage of development and dealing with the same issues we are. We experience a different kind of pleasure, the pleasure of *intimacy*. We learn to confide, trust, consider, accept and understand. We have an expanding experience of 'other' and the challenge of fitting in with that other.

The third pleasure phase starts at adolescence or puberty. This is the experience of *sexuality*, and it's a mind-blowing event. We have new and strange urges, bodily changes which are accompanied by self-exploration and discovery. This is accompanied by an emerging awareness of the opposite sex and realisation of their physical differences.

We're no longer androgynous or neutral, but are clearly male or female. This magical mystery tour is often accompanied by touching, petting 'making out'. We're introduced to physical sensations that are intense and enjoyable. How satisfying, appropriate and developed these three phases are will determine the quality of our overall sensual ability to relate and be a good lover.

For an adult lover, the easiest of the three to master is sex. What's necessary is experience and experiment. This is the mechanics, the nuts and bolts, nitty-gritty of love-making. What goes where, when and how. We owe it to ourselves and to prospective partners to know our bodies well, what turns us on and what's necessary for our sexual pleasure. We should learn how to achieve orgasm. There are sex manuals like the classic *Joy Of Sex* by Alex Comfort and countless others. We need to take responsibility for our own sexual well-being. We need to be willing to communicate about our sexuality with our partners.

Often a woman will complain about her lover's inadequacies and ineptness. When I ask her if she's told him, she'll say, 'If he were a good lover, he'd know.' Not fair! He may be the world's best lover but worst mind-reader. Honesty in sex may be awkward but it's necessary. Accentuate the positive, what they're doing right, but be tactfully frank about what's not working. Sometimes it's helpful to demonstrate on yourself, or to physically guide your partner as to what to do for you.

Resentment is the stuff that makes relationships come unstuck and it's the stuff that can determine the difference between putting your sex life on a downhill slide or being willing to communicate and turn sex into Olympic gold medal material.

Males tend to be more physically sexual and women more psychologically sexual. It is my secret belief that on the seventh day, instead of resting, God manifested his sense of humour by putting men's sexuality in their genitals and women's in their heads. A very common disaster in long-term relationships is something I call the 'on-duty vagina' syndrome. This is where the embers of the romancing and wooing, necessary for winning the chase, have long since turned to ash.

As stated earlier, women respond best sexually when they feel *real*ised, made to feel real. A woman likes to think that the man she's with sexually knows the 'her that lives inside her'. How often I hear the complaint 'My husband hasn't said a nice thing to me in days, hasn't complimented me in weeks, hasn't acknowledged anything I've accomplished in months and all of a sudden he has an erection and I'm supposed to do something about it. He wonders why I'm not interested!'

The greatest complaint I receive from men concerning sexual wet blanketism is the annoying habit women have of putting men down. 'There I am in a romantic, sexual mood, feeling warm and loving, and all of a sudden I get hit with a barrage of what I've done wrong for the past six days, months, years. She may feel better for having got it off her chest, but the last thing I feel is loving!'

Occasionally, we all need to lift our game and ask ourselves, 'If this were a date, would we score?'

Affection is important in a good lover. This is asexual *not* sexual touching. It is what you do with your cat while watching television. This has to feel safe and must not be mistaken for sexual foreplay. (How many times have I heard female partners say, 'If I ask you to hug me, please don't ... me.') This is the form of pleasuring that replaces the feelings we had as children with our parents. It makes us feel nurtured, taken care of, pampered. It allows us a feeling of 'stop the world, I want to get off' and for a while feel carefree and childlike.

Intimacy is the third ingredient that makes a good lover. This element is one partners most often complain is missing in their lover. It is the most misunderstood, underachieved and most sensual aspect of love-making. The best way to describe intimacy is to imagine a circle, about two metres in diameter. You and your partner are safely cocooned within the circle. Everyone and everything else is outside this magic circle, where masks, make-up and facades are unnecessary.

- This is where either partner can say, 'I feel safe to be my real self with you.'
- Where I can tell you my innermost secrets and trust that they will never be used against me. And I can invite you to do the same.
- Where I can share with you what I can't share with friends or even my family, and have you share those things with me.
- Where I can tell you that you hurt me and not be afraid you will be angry at me, but will want to know why, and I can invite you to share your feelings too.
- Where you will be stronger than I am when I need you to be, where it feels safe for you to tell me something I don't want to hear but need to know, and you won't judge me.
- Where I can say that I feel scared, ashamed, angry, sad, humiliated and nothing bad will happen to me, and you can also say these things.
- Where you make me feel you want to know the 'me that lives inside me', and when you know that me, you will protect, support and befriend that me. That you will be on my side.

Such a circle is intimate, sexy, sensual.

How do you rate? Ask your partner. Have them evaluate you in each of the three categories. Make it clear that you invite, want, insist on honesty. Take turns. In a category where you're lacking, you'll feel strange, self-conscious, embarrassed. You'll have to push against your inhibitions. Be willing to feel silly, awkward and uncomfortable. The uncomfortable feelings won't last. Keep asking for and giving feedback. Don't be defensive.

Remember that courage is the willingness to be afraid and act anyway. The reward should be an amazing, successful and sensual relationship. You and your partner are able to say he or she's my sexual mate, my nurturer, my best friend. You will also know that when it comes to being great lovers, you're up there with the masters.

Getting Women Right

In my many years of practice, there is a complaint that seems never-ending and gender-biased. 'I don't get enough sex' would have to be at least two to one a male, as opposed to a female, grievance. The thing is, I'm rarely surprised by the men for whom this is a gripe. I'm not being catty here. God knows I don't hold myself up as a litmus test of who's sexy and who's not. There's no accounting for human taste. But in most of these cases, I would pass if offered a sexual encounter with them as well.

What would happen if we pretended there were no such thing as female sexual autonomy, that we were sexually inert? In other words, what would it be like if our sexuality had no independent life force of its own. There it is, a dormant possibility. And the prize goes to the male who figures out what it takes to activate the engine.

What some men lack is an understanding of the psychology of female sexuality. And look, I'm not blaming them, women are difficult creatures to understand at the best of times. Sexually, we're a minefield. What I want to zero in on is marital or long-term sex. This is about a man and a woman who had a good sex life once, but the flame went out.

I'd like a dollar for every case I've handled where the husband complains that his wife is totally uninterested in sex, and it unfolds that she's having a torrid affair with someone else. It turns out that it's not that she's unable to be turned on, she's just not turned on by *him*. I'd love to interview the partner of the male who came up with the diagnosis 'frigid'.

The worst scenario of sexual breakdown is the extreme case where a woman complains that her husband is often angry, berating or cranky. Sometimes he behaves as though he doesn't even respect, let alone like her. Yet when he gets horny he expects her to service his need. And he wonders why she's not interested! She says she feels like a sexual object. It appears to her that any female with the right equipment would do. It certainly doesn't feel like what's going on has anything to do with her.

Nothing is a greater turn-off than feeling as though your body is being used as the solution to someone else's sexual problem.

A good lover is the man who claims he'd rather not have sex at all than have it with a partner who's not interested. He'd rather wait until she is. The irony of this is that there's nothing he could do that is more intimate, enticing or sexy than to show this sensitivity. This respect for her needs raises the probability of her wanting sex by quantum leaps. It takes an enormous amount of unselfishness and maturity to do this, and a willingness to know his partner intimately. His reward is usually a wonderful sex life.

If a couple had a sexual relationship that worked at one time, what this means is that he once knew how to be considerate, how to meet her needs and how to be intimate. When he was courting or seducing, it was necessary for him to put in the effort and to take the time *then*. Is it that men get lazy or think it no longer matters? Does he think that now that he's 'got her', she'll run on auto-pilot indefinitely.

Fellas, think back to those good old days. This is what you must have known. Flirting works. When a man who understands female sexuality is looking for a partner, what he knows is that he's going to have to study her enough to make her think that he sees through to her inner self. Then he's going to have to prove to her that he understands her by what he says or does. Intimacy aids in making her feel there's more about her he's attracted to than just her body. Even reflective listening works. 'In other words what you're saying is ...' Or, 'I can see that must have been upsetting for you,' 'From what you're saying it sounds like ...'

Compliments work, as long as they're accurate and true. 'You have the most expressive green eyes I've ever seen' won't work if her eyes are brown! I've had men say they can't believe women fall for those lines. They do, as long as they know they're sincere and genuine. Only the most naive woman believes construction site catcalls are a personal tribute.

Does this mean that I'm promoting sleaze, Don Juanism or insincerity? No. But first things first. Expertise at seduction is first and foremost an art. There's nothing wrong with mastering the skills of romance, flirtation and intimacy. To use those skills as a means of exploiting and manipulating is irresponsible. What I'm suggesting is developing the ability to enhance an already established relationship.

I think a little lateral thinking is called for. Just imagine what it would be like if it became the accepted social standard that men 'got' what they deserved. Yup. Just suppose for a minute that the onus of responsibility for how much sex a male got was totally his.

Picture a male around a motorbike, a car, a boat. If 'she' doesn't turn over, he'll concentrate, he'll listen, he'll tinker and fiddle until he has 'her' purring like a kitten. Picture a dinner party. She says, 'Poor Harold, he hasn't been "getting much" lately.' And as *his* face reddens, the blokes think to themselves, 'gee, she doesn't look that hard to operate,' and the women commiserate with her unfortunate circumstances, being stuck with such an unmechanically-minded, ill-adept bungler. And pigs might fly.

P.S. In all fairness, anyone who reads newspapers will have noticed the ever-increasing deluge of advertisements for male impotency clinics. Certainly, sexual dysfunction is not a unilateral issue. As I discussed earlier, I think women also need to take note of men's needs and feelings and provide more support for their gender validation. I hope I've given fair treatment to the case for not cutting off our noses to spite our faces (no phallic symbolism intended).

All in the FAMILY

Relationships almost never exist in a vacuum. There are always the ripple effects caused by other family members who impact on our primary partnerships. I've included a few of the more common folks and situations that are particularly difficult to handle. With step families and single parent families ever more on the increase, and teens 'doing their own thing', it can make family politics increasingly difficult. Getting this network of relationships right goes a long way towards safeguarding the sanctity of a partnership without letting outside, potentially polarising issues become destructive.

Mum and Dad, Meet Kylie

'She walked in, sat down and helped herself to whatever she wanted in our refrigerator, felt free to borrow a jumper out of our daughter's wardrobe, and spray herself with Chanel No. 5 from the bottle on my wife's dressing table; all without asking.

'"My name is Kylie, as in Minogue," she drawled in a pouty, pseudo-sexy voice, ending in the puckering of her bright red, pencilled-in lips. It made us all want to puke, except for our son, Mitchell. He thinks he's won the lottery. He cannot believe his luck.

'My wife and I thought he'd never outgrow his matey, football stage and find a woman he thought as attractive as his teammates, beer and sweatshirted, blokey weekends. When he said he had a surprise to bring home to meet us, we were prepared to dance a highland fling. Mitchell was coming of age, he was about to have a reason to change his smelly, sweaty socks, dump his Neanderthal phase and grow up.

'"Mum and Dad," he said, "I'd like you to meet Kylie." She had legs that went all the way up. This was partly because her skirt barely covered her bottom. Her leather halter-neck top didn't cover much more. I felt like putting a blindfold on our impressionable thirteen-year-old daughter. She used her fork as though she were trying to get more staccato out of the bassoon section. It wasn't so much snobbiness on our parts, but a reaction to her complete lack of manners and consideration. We kept thinking she just wasn't good enough.

'Look, I'm not a dinosaur. I remember my first sexual relationship. I was addicted to my girlfriend. But I always had the feeling it was a rite-of-passage relationship, that it was a step into manhood and the rest of my life. I knew we were both too young to settle down. And she was a suitable candidate to be a life partner. Kylie is so obviously not. What do we do? Do we tell him the way we feel?'

Sound familiar?

What I tell the father, Allen, is that I've been asked the same question a hundred times. The answer varies, depending on the relationship the parents have with their children.

I had a client who ran a virtual matriarchy. She had a daughter over whom she wielded a great deal of control. Over the years her daughter lost confidence in her own decision-making abilities because she didn't do much without her mother putting in her two cents' worth. When she brought home 'the one', her mother made an 'over my dead body' edict. The prospective suitor was a brickie, not a barrister.

The daughter dutifully obeyed. She also became chronically depressed. She ended up marrying a barrister who passed muster, but with whom she was never happy. After seven years of marriage, they divorced. Her relationship with her mother had long since soured. She always resented her for interfering with her decision to marry the brickie, with whom she believed she would have been happy.

The mother won her selected son-in-law, but lost her daughter.

Another client, who had a close relationship with his son, had some strong reservations about his son's chosen partner. He felt she was a user and feared she would take what she could from his son, but not contribute to his needs. He asked his son to help him with a new lawn he was putting in. He waited until they'd spent a day together, then, when they were relaxing over a beer, he told his son what his concerns were. The son said he'd never seen what his father had seen. He said he'd be on the lookout to see if he could perceive what he meant. He did and soon broke off the relationship. He was forever grateful to his father for sharing his insight.

In another case, both parents thought their daughter was making a mistake. They suspected the man had violent tendencies, but felt if they said anything to their rebellious daughter, their comments would push their daughter even closer to her chosen partner. Instead they prayed she'd wake up and not go through with the wedding. She didn't. She went ahead with it. She didn't leave him until she landed in hospital with concussion, a black eye and a broken rib. She admitted that even if her parents had said something she would have gone through with it. She thought she could change him and had to learn the hard way that she couldn't.

Most children want parental approval, but at the same time they want to see themselves as independent adults, capable of working out their own choices and deciding their own fate.

So, what do you do if you see your child walking into a disaster area?

One technique is to do your homework before the issue arises. Ask your children whether or not they want your input and opinion on future partners they may introduce you to. This sets up a policy of permission for you to communicate your feelings when the time comes.

If it's too late and the seemingly unworthy heart-throb is already on the scene, you can still ask if your two cents' worth is wanted. If they say yes, all is well. If they say no, then you have to back off, but you've planted a seed. They know you would never have asked the question unless there was something on your mind. Curiosity most often gets the better of them. They'll want to know what they haven't seen. They'll be curious to know if it's something they've missed or something they already know that doesn't bother them.

Another technique is to have a general discussion that is philosophical and objective about your concern: 'I read an article the other day . . . I have a friend who has a daughter . . . I heard about this woman who got into an abusive relationship. What do you think about that?' or, 'How would you act if a friend of yours was in an abusive relationship? Do you think your friend would thank you for telling her how you feel or not?' You can take your lead from their reaction. Or just let your child think about it.

Be prepared to give your opinion, then drop it. Our children need to know that it's their life, their decision. The less judgment we pass and the more freedom we give them, the more permission they can give themselves to change their minds. Freedom of choice is the feeling they really are free to do what they choose. Then, if they don't proceed, they'll know it was their decision, not the result of manipulation or a parent pleaser.

With divorce rates indicating that one in three marriages will reach an untimely end, the one relationship that can't be replaced is that of the parent and child. Ultimately, we may not have much control over their partnerships, but no matter what happens between our children and their mates, it's important their relationship with us remains intact.

Finally, if we remember back, we see that, just as it was impossible for anyone to have our experiences for us, as much as we'd like to, it's impossible for us to have our children's negative experiences for them. It just can't be done.

Whether you call them mistakes or experience, ultimately the getting of wisdom is about sorting out what does and doesn't work for us. At a recent women's function, one participant asked the sixteen of us for a show of hands. 'How many of us are still on first husbands?' Three hands were held up. Even though most of us had got it wrong the first time, we all managed to learn by our mistakes. Examining what didn't work for us made it clearer what would work in the future. We'd all remarried and could report happy outcomes.

Wanting to protect your children is part of parenthood. Wanting to be proud of your children is understandable. But what about when those feelings go beyond pride to become possession?

'My Little Man' and 'Daddy's Little Princess'

The thing that proctologists and mothers have in common is that they are both in chosen professions they're not allowed to talk about. The difference between them is that proctologists know this.

I have one group of friends who are now at an age where the topic has switched to grandchildren. I made plans to go away with them for a long weekend. Sally's been friends with them for over forty years and is childless. She's the one with whom I decided to discuss my predicament, because I knew she wouldn't take it personally.

'Sally, what do you advise I do about this weekend? The topic of children and grandchildren bores me witless.'

'If you think the subject bothers you, what about me? I'm not childless by choice. I've had to put up with "baby talk" my whole adult life. It distresses me every time. Firstly, as a reminder of what I'll never have and secondly, their insensitivity hurts.'

I'd never looked at it from that angle. I have children. Sally's perspective just added moral indignation to what was already a cause based on the tedium of the topic.

Here's what we came up with. At dinner on Friday, I announced I had a challenge. The rules for the weekend were that no-one was allowed to tell an offspring story unless it was newsworthy enough to be printed in *WHO* magazine. Any slip-ups would cost the offender $5 to go towards the cost of lunch on Monday.

Some found it really hard. It was like watching people suffering nicotine withdrawal. It was not uncommon to see someone open their mouth to speak, think twice, then close it. By the end of the weekend, there was only one transgression committed by the worst offender. As a reminder we let the penalty stand. She took it good-heartedly, because another thing she discovered about herself was that, independent of the subject of her successful daughter, she has a lot to contribute.

We learned things about each other we'd never known. The conversations were interesting, revealing and intimate. Joan confessed a secret desire for her grandchildren to reach an age where she was no longer needed to babysit. She'd love to go to TAFE and take a gardening course. Joan decided to split the babysitting cost with her daughter and is now landscaping madly.

This newly imposed rule established a precedent for the future. Our get-togethers now have a freshness, a new vitality, and I look forward to them.

Professional mothers. They're easily recognised. They often start off a topic of conversation with 'my', then fill in the child's name. They refer to their children as though they were appendages. We're not talking unintelligent here. This peculiarity transcends economic, social and academic boundaries. One of the most seriously afflicted 'mothers' I know is a successful pathologist, another is a research scientist.

What about the offspring of these mothers? You'd think they'd love all the doting attention they receive, but what I have found, working with them in therapy, is a real love/hate relationship. Sure, anybody would like to be the object of so much affection, but it often goes beyond affection into something that feels to them a lot more like possessiveness.

The children complain that they feel dominated. They have trouble perceiving themselves as adults. It's like an umbilical cord that never gets cut. They are left with the love of the closeness, but a real resentment of the possessiveness. These children talk about feeling strangled. They express guilt over treacherous thoughts of a need for independence. When among friends who fawn over their children in public, I've watched their children squirm and roll their eyes with discomfort.

What about the husbands? When there's been a marriage breakdown, I try to track down the start of the unhappiness. More times than I'd like to count, it will turn out to be from the time of the birth of a child.

Husbands talk about feeling abandoned, that sex stops, that they've lost their partner to their child. With possessive mothers, there's often jealousy over the child's attention. The mother traditionally has had the time advantage over the working father. As the mother/child relationship develops, often the husband feels like there's a club operating in his home of which he is not a member. Over a period of time this isolation takes its toll, estranging husband from wife, and father from child.

What about the mothers? Is their devotion a blind spot? Is

it that because they are so interested in their children, they think others will find the topic as interesting? Or is it something else?

Are their children meant to serve a purpose? Sometimes they can provide a way of fulfilling expectations the mother felt she failed to live up to. She can attain through her children the glory she never achieved herself. Children can be an excuse for not living one's own life.

Children can also be an insurance policy against loneliness in old age and a substitute partner in an unfulfilling, cold marriage. In the motherhood role, the woman can initiate and be in control of the affection, intimacy and closeness.

The role of motherhood is such a significant one that it's important to get it right. Here are some questions you can ask yourself:

- Who would I be if I didn't have children?
- Are my children a solution to anything unfulfilled in my life?
- Am I giving them messages that if they ever separated from me, I'd be devastated?
- Are my children my answer to my unhappy marriage?
- Can I be alone?
- Are my children meant to hide my insecurities?
- Is it my intention to teach my children life skills so they can end up independent adults?

If the answers don't tally, panic not. Most mothers have at one time or another questioned their motherhood motives. This does not indicate signs of *Mommie Dearest.* But it might be a good idea to have a chat with your children, if they're old enough, about how they perceive you as a mother. If your children are young and you can see that your relationship with them might smack of possessiveness or dependence, talk to your husband or a counsellor — for their sake, your husband's sake and, most importantly, for your own sake.

If none of the above pertains to you as a mother, then I'm going to tell you something your best friend won't. The topic of your children is of interest only to your immediate family, your children's school teachers, your paediatrician, auntys and uncles and to no-one else. If people ask you about them, they are merely being polite. They don't really want to know, or they want to know in the amount of time it would take if they asked how your chrysanthemums are coming along. Trust me.

The 'My Little Mate' syndrome, attributable to fathers, is not as punishing to the listening audience. Its effects are seemingly more scarring to the little mate.

I'm talking about the brigade of dads seen on the sidelines at sporting events. In some cases, their screams of encouragement have an undercurrent of threat, criticism and ego extension. You have a sense that it wouldn't be fun to be a part of their post-game wrap-up.

Mothers have been accused of basking in their children's glory; fathers seem far more threatened by being associated with their progenies (especially their sons) failures. If there is a socially difficult situation in a household, often the child confides in the mother, whose unconditional love seems more assured. The mother's job is to then temper the material and try to present it in some palatable form to the father. I'm talking about everything from long hair, to school failures to the issue of homosexuality. Whereas both parents are fond of bragging about their children's victories, fathers have a tough time treating their children as separate people from themselves when it comes to perceived failures. They tend to take it personally.

Fathers can find it difficult to cross the line from instructor to intimate friend or equal. It's like they don't know how to communicate unless they're in the role of teacher, and this way of acting can become habitual. Often a child misinterprets this as never-ending criticism when in fact it's an inability to switch gears and change roles. Adult mother/offspring friendships seem to come easier than father/offspring relationships.

In the United States, there is a national organisation called S.O.Bs. The letters stand for 'Sons of Bosses'. Often the son is more educated and sometimes more capable than his father was, but the father has trouble changing his perception of his 'little mate' to that of peer.

This ineptness in the role change from authority figure to friend also exists between father and daughter. 'Daddy's little Princess' is OK until boys come into the picture. Then the father flashes back to what was on his mind when he was a teenager and imagines all kinds of woeful sexual outcomes. Steve Martin did a good job of portraying this dilemma in *Father of the Bride*. Some fathers have trouble realising Daddy's little girl has grown up. Again, if she doesn't *need* him, who is he supposed to be to her?

There is also a uniquely paternal phenomenon of com-petition for supremacy and leader of the pack which occurs between fathers and sons. This often starts at adolescence, when the father realises that his days of being the stronger of the household males is under threat. I have often heard the sad tale of a son receiving physical abuse from a father. The son restrains himself out of respect, but once he realises he is big enough to hit back it usually marks the time for the son to leave the household.

There are of course, many fathers who are able to bridge the stages of teacher, authority figure and role model, to become friend, adviser and supporter. They offer one of the most rewarding, important and powerful relationships a child and a father can have.

Teenagers — a Therapist's Nightmare

Picture the scene. The year: 1962. The place: Harvard Square, Cambridge, Massachusetts. The occasion: an anti-Vietnam rally. Cast of characters: assorted, youthful, self-righteous students including Dr Barron's daughter. Dressed in jeans, black turtle-neck, loose shoulder-length hair, no make-up, black eyeliner, thonged sandals and carrying a 'MAKE LOVE NOT WAR' placard, marching stridently down the main street, bellowing 'We Shall Overcome'. From a parental point of view, I was a fully fledged, hippy horror story. Furthermore, I'm afraid it's genetic.

Last year, when one of my sons, the lead singer with the rock group the Spin Doctors, was out here on tour from America, a reporter asked me what it was like being the mother of a famous rock star. Without a millisecond of thought, I said, 'Being the mother of a famous rock star means never having to say I'm sorry about the way he looks.' Christopher wasn't always a rock star and the only concession I could ever get him to make concerning his dress code was for his grandmother, and that was under duress. But hey, I know. These days if a parent's only complaint is their teen's attire, they have a lot to be grateful for.

There wouldn't be many therapists these days who wouldn't have at least one case of parents who have a teen from Hell who's left home and headed for the Kings Cross of their big city. It's epidemic.

This is the story of Christos and Sue Smith. He's a film producer and she's a teacher. They have three children: daughter eighteen, daughter sixteen, son fifteen. Sue delayed her study until the youngest was in school full-time and she chose teaching so she could be home around the same time as the kids.

Christos and Sue believed the family that played together, stayed together. They holidayed as a family and actively involved themselves in their children's interests. Elenie, the sixteen-year-old, was committed to rowing, which pleased Christos because he was also a keen rower. He got up at 5.00 o'clock every morning to take Elenie to training. She competed state-wide. He was her greatest fan.

When the principal of Elenie's school called Christos and Sue in for a conference, they were concerned and anxious. Anxiety soon turned to horror with her disclosure that Elenie had for some time been leading a double life. It had started when she met some kids at the train station on her way to school. These kids hung around there as they wagged school, smoked dope, shoplifted and generally cruised. The scene appealed to Elenie so she had joined them.

In a nightmare odyssey that followed, Elenie quit school and rowing, ran away, got into drugs, a graffiti gang, got pregnant and had an abortion. What got her home was an event where she and her group robbed a liquor store. In their escape, the shopkeeper caught Elenie and bashed her senseless. She revealed her parents' name in the emergency room.

When her mother brought her to my office, she had clearly dressed for the occasion. She was wearing a grossly oversized outfit — St. Vincent's finest. A tuft of orange hair stood out from her otherwise brunette mane. And when she crossed her legs, two things happened. First, she revealed a shoe with only the heel connected to the main frame. The toe part of the sole gaped open. Secondly, I began to laugh. Petulance turned to curiosity. 'What's so funny?' she asked. 'I'm just admiring your attention to detail,' I answered. 'I couldn't have done a better job myself. I think your get-up is fabulous.' And so counselling began.

From a therapist's point of view, the difficulty in treating wayward adolescents is threefold: 1. The *problem* is they're driving their parents nuts, which is exactly their intention. 2. They didn't book the appointment because in fact, *they* don't have a problem. 3. They don't pay for it.

The only leverage a therapist has is to gain the teenager's respect. Then they should concede that the teen has achieved their objective, although they've also painted themselves into a corner. Their parents are sufficiently traumatised and punished for their perceived sin of 'high expectations', 'too strict', 'don't understand me', 'domineering', etc, but the price of this vengeance life-wise is that the kid's a loser, on a nowhere trip towards nothing and nowhere. What's needed is a dose of life ownership. In umpteen years time their parents will be dead, then who will the knocking off of liquor stores be directed at?

One revelation that really gets up teenage noses is a fact these liberated, free-spirited rebels fail to see: they're robots. What they're rebelling against are the 'straights', so they become the opposite. They're simply mirror images. Equally predictable. Flip side, same coin. I point out that if I were their parent and I wanted them to move to the left, I'd simply instruct them to move to the right. Piece of cake.

I ask the question, 'Why do you think your parents have high expectations, are demanding and overly instructive?' If I'm dealing with an ill-behaved but honest teen, I can almost always get them to admit that the answer is because their parents love them. They know that on a deep level but are more in touch with their crankiness about *how* they're being loved.

So what advice can be given about teenage management? It helps enormously if you don't fall into the classic 'parent role' trap which starts at the birth of the first child. How many of us have friends, dear friends, who are wonderful, intelligent, spontaneous and perceptive. Then they have a child, don a parent hat and act like they've had a frontal lobotomy.

They speak to their children in a way they speak to no-one else. Sometimes before our very eyes, in the middle of a conversation with us, they'll have an aside to one of their progeny in a totally different tone of voice. Parent voice. Kids are short people but that doesn't make them stupid. They have sensitive snifters for people who are role-playing. What this does is put you out of relationship with them. You stand a better chance of a good relationship if you dare to be real.

Think back to the first time you realised *your* parents didn't have all the answers. For me it was at age eight. There was a rule about school shoes and party shoes. The problem was wanting to wear the party shoes to school. Solution: smuggle them and don't forget to change back. Sad but true, by the time they're seven, eight or nine we've lost our grip. If you're willing to come to terms with that, the rest is pretty simple.

'Mum, can I drive down to the snow with Bill?' 'Alex, I don't want you to drive that far with him because it's a long way and there may be icy conditions. He's only been driving for a month. I'm perfectly aware I can't stop you if you decide to go, but I'd prefer you didn't.'

This lets Alex know that you don't approve, what your reasons are and that you acknowledge you have no power over him. Kids like guidance, approval and to feel in control of their lives and choices. It doesn't guarantee he won't go, but it raises the odds. In an adversarial negotiation where someone wins and someone loses, you reduce the odds of a positive outcome.

Be real, but also be realistic. Let's say Alex decides to go to the snow with Bill. How would you feel? Angry, disappointed, not liking him very much? Express that in your behaviour towards him. Put yourself 'out of relationship' with him. This is a subtle but powerful technique. It's not ignoring or the silent treatment.

If you've ever had the bad luck to spend time around a person who is totally self-absorbed, you'll know what I mean. You can talk to them, but you know their mind is elsewhere. You feel like knocking on their head and saying, 'Hello. Is anybody home in there?' They aren't really rude or aggressive or being nasty. They're distracted and vacant, not connected or in communication with you. If you're going to get through, you're going to have to try hard.

Take a page out of their book. That is the look you want. The intention is to make the recipient feel as though they're in the same room as you, but in solitary confinement. This is far more effective than punishment or a lecture. He's temporarily lost you, and the responsibility of rectifying the relationship is his. They like approval. He'll come around.

Finally, teen-wise, partner-wise, life-wise, it's better to go for the respect vote instead of the popularity vote. Parents who get that wrong look weak, crawling and pathetic to us *and* to their kids. While your children are growing up, they don't need you to be their best friend. They should have age-appropriate friends. They need you to be their guide, role model, support and mentor.

Whatever happened to Elenie? I bumped into her socially at her father's fortieth birthday party. She was wearing a dress covered with flowers. Her hair was pulled back with ribbon. She'd finished her HSC and had worked to save enough to go overseas.

But this isn't Disneyworld and it doesn't always have a happy ending. There are teens who are so peer-oriented, rebellious, destructive and unmanageable that the only option is to take firm action, especially where there are siblings in the household. If their behaviour is so disruptive that it impinges on the rights of other family members, sometimes it becomes necessary to lock out the offending teenager. In the States, this is called 'hard love'.

Insist they find alternative accommodation until they comply with household standards of behaviour. Don't make it personal. 'I understand your need for individual expression, but it's too disruptive for the rest of us. As soon as you can return as a cooperative citizen, we'd love to welcome you back. We hope it won't take long.' This puts the responsibility for their behaviour in their hands, leaves out judgment and lets them know that if they comply, the door is always open.

Growing up. It appears some of us are just destined to stop and make a statement along the way. Some glide into adulthood, others lurch. When parents say about their children, 'I just want them to be happy,' that's partially altruism speaking. The other part is that when they finally are happy or at least settled, we can put our feet up, breathe a sigh of relief and say glory hallelujah! At last the job is done.

The Unkindest
Cut of All

Any student of psychology will tell you that from the day we open our books and travel from Freud to Adler through Jung to graduation day, there is a definite skew in our science that leans towards a cause and effect paradigm. Very simply, the cause is the parent, the effect is the child. If the parents get it wrong, their children will become our customers. If they get it right, their children will be contenders for the cover of *Mental Health* magazine. I invite those theorists to sit next to me some days.

Gloria has a son who is twenty-four. She and her husband Bruce planned for his birth and anticipated his arrival with excitement. They were the usual first-time parents, bursting with the secret information that they were in possession of the only perfect child ever born. Bruce was a hands-on father. Gloria was a trained nurse who gave up work to be there for their son, Tim. She nurtured, she listened, she advised, she consoled and she managed the house.

When Tim left home, she always had his telephone number. When missing him became too much, she'd pick up the phone and make contact. Once she called only to have a recording say, 'This phone has been disconnected. Please check the number you are dialling.' Gloria knew Tim was planning a move but she didn't know it had already happened.

Bruce had been dissatisfied with Tim's behaviour. He had been feeling for a long time that Tim's response was coming up way short of what Gloria gave him and he felt her efforts were being taken for granted. He'd attempted to talk to Tim about it but didn't think he'd made much headway. He advised Gloria not to chase him and see how long it would take him to make contact if left to his own devices. Three months passed. She booked in to see me. The pain was terrible.

She said she grieved for the dream of what she thought her relationship with Tim was, as opposed to what it actually has turned out to be. He hadn't been a terribly affectionate child, but she felt her vast amount of affection was enough for both of them. He'd never freely said 'I love you'.

He'd only respond, 'You too, Mum or Dad.' When there were school outings or summer camp, and later, a year overseas, they fretted more about the separations than Tim did.

Parents are there to give, not to receive, she thought. It never occurred to her she should look for anything in return. She rationalised that he was asserting his independence. He had a life of his own to lead. He was busy. It didn't occur to her that if she stopped driving the relationship, she would see it had no life force of its own.

Gloria had passed through the shock of realisation. She didn't even take Tim personally. In the way that Tim loves, he loved them. She saw that he was, and had always been, caught up in his own reality. He didn't take much notice of anyone outside of himself except when they affected him. It wasn't selfishness as much as a lack of awareness of others. She assumed all children were that way and they grew out of it. The truth was emerging that at twenty-four he probably was the way he was always going to be.

The real problem was that she didn't know who or how to be around him, now that being all-giving, all-loving and all-attentive was too much and over the top.

This is about parents for whom their children simply have no chemistry.

Parents who aren't careless plan for the advent of children because it is what they want — children, a family. There is a nine-month incubation period where the parents develop a relationship with the unborn foetus. Often this relationship is stronger with the mother because the relationship is ceaseless. This fantasised relationship is born out of what children and family mean to the parents. The child isn't there to vote yet. It is born with all the anticipation of what it is meant to fulfil in the parents' script. Is this wrong? It's unavoidable.

The greatest disappointment comes when the parents' expectations and the child's personality are in conflict. It is also the greatest source of loss and confusion for the parent when the preconceived picture doesn't live up to the dream. At the very least there is the expectation that in exchange for the creativity of life there will be the sharing of that life with its creators.

What do you do when a heart full of love from one evokes a sense of obligation from the other? In these cases, the problem is that the parent perpetually feels towards the child the excitement one would towards a new lover. The child feels towards the parent as one does towards a neighbour for whom he feels an affinity but whom he could easily live without. The feelings of rejection are tough going for the parent.

What is hereditary and what isn't is a debate that has raged from time immemorial. It has always been my belief there are certain personality traits people have that are innate. I have a friend who divides all humankind into the 'warms' and the 'colds'. They are who they are from birth. We parents were simply the vehicle that delivered them.

Parenting is about affording safe journey onto the planet and then acting responsibly in our decision to procreate by doing the right thing by the child. The task is to educate children into the ability to flee the coop into responsible lives. Job done.

In schools today, educators are aware of the diagnosis of the nineties — 'attention deficit disorder'. This diagnosis is the child of 'hyperactive' syndrome and the grandchild of 'dyslexia'. What became apparent was that there were children with reading difficulties who had trouble focusing and concentrating for long periods of time. With therapy this disability could be remedied.

I wonder if, one day, children might be tested for a different kind of perceptual disability, the inability to focus on 'another'. There are millions of children who become adults who have absolutely no concept of what goes on outside the environs of their own skin. They process all reality in terms of 'this is good for me', or 'this is bad for me'. What is happening to people around them or how their behaviour impacts on others is a complete blind spot.

How to advise Gloria? The answer is to lower the love volume and energy level directed towards Tim to match his level. Gloria's imbalance of outgoing love may be a turn-off. He may sense there is too big an ask back by the amount of her emotional investment. If she backs off he may find her more inviting.

The other thing this will do is give Gloria back her self-respect. It will give her a sense of self-empowerment, so she doesn't see herself as impotently always at his beck and call. It will stop Tim taking her love for granted. When and if he notices the quiet or void that will exist, he may be motivated to take the driver's seat in the relationship. With a major fan's applause missing from the audience, he may take notice and start performing better.

If it doesn't happen now, there's a possibility that the reconciliation could take place when Tim has a child of his own. This is when he will have an experience of being at the whim of his own child and know first-hand how tenuous the relationship is on the parental receiving end. Unfortunately, the other significant time when the need to connect may manifest is when a child hits middle age and starts to contemplate their own mortality. If their parents are still alive there can be a drive to reconcile, before it's too late.

Tragically, for a lot of parents who have not only done the right thing, but have done everything they can for their child, the best relationship they may ever have with the child is the one they had with the unborn foetus. The unkindest cut of all can be the umbilical cord. Kids — they can be bad value for the effort, the time and the money.

But there are other people, besides parents, who may end up being rejected, particularly if a family break-up has occurred.

Disenfranchised Grandparents

C olin and Maisy are in their late sixties. They have come to see me because their next-door neighbour thought talking to someone might make them feel better. Maisy has pulled a handkerchief out of her handbag. She's twisting its crocheted border. She's not crying. The hankie's there just in case. Colin looks acutely uncomfortable. He's from the generation who think anyone who can't sort out their own problems might as well put a bullet through their heads. He's there for Maisy.

After he fought in the Second World War, Colin returned to the workforce. He joined a bank, became a manager in a small town and worked his way up to regional and national level. He did all right for himself and provided well for Maisy and their only child, Simon. Maisy wanted more children but it just didn't turn out that way.

Simon was sent to boarding school where he did well. After graduation he went on to university and obtained a business degree. He's now an executive with a computer company. Along the way he married Clare, a school teacher, and they have two children, Matthew and Beth.

Colin and Maisy were fond of Clare and the birth of their grandchildren was a great joy to them both. It also coincided with Colin's retirement. Along with golf, taking Matthew fishing became a favourite hobby. A close bond developed between the grandparents and their grandchildren.

The grandparents looked after the children any time they were asked, which was fairly often because both Simon and Clare were in prime professional achievement mode. Matthew and Beth would come up to Colin and Maisy's beach cottage during the summer school holidays. The four of them looked forward to it all year.

Matthew and Beth were nine and seven when Simon announced that he was leaving Clare for another woman. The other woman was a work colleague. She was the receptionist at Simon's office.

Simon had reached that peculiar and increasingly common male phase where he felt that what would best accessorise his Armani suit was someone in white, spangled boots who had aspirations to be a rock star and was eighteen years younger than him.

To say it wasn't a friendly divorce is to say it would make the *War Of The Roses* look like the cartoon before the main feature.

The ordeal left Clare as bitter and twisted as a chilli-flavoured pretzel. Out of guilt, Simon was happy to make a very generous financial settlement, so the only revenge Clare could take was in the custody and access area. On the grounds that she thought Simon's behaviour was demonstrably immoral, she tried to disallow him any access to the children.

Clare was granted custody and Simon was allowed alternate weekend access. Clare never spoke to him except when it involved the children, nor to any member of his family, including her in-laws.

Simon was now caught in a three-ring circus. His children couldn't help but be influenced by their mother's acrimony so they always started their weekends with their father with an attitude which called for patience and time on Simon's part.

The new girlfriend was less than pleased to be upstaged at the best of times. She didn't like Simon's children and the feeling was mutual. Blood being thicker than water, Colin and Maisy tried to adjust to this crisis in their lives the best way they knew how, but they had very little in common with a young, aspiring rock star. She mistook their awkwardness for dislike, so she had little time for his 'oldies' as well.

Simon could have ended up auditioning for centre ring in Ashton's Circus, keeping all five balls in the air. He tried hard but something had to give. Colin and Maisy became the victims of low-end priority.

Clare ended up settling with a man in another state. He and Clare had a child together. Now there was another set of grandparents, pushing Colin and Maisy further into the background.

At the time of writing, Colin and Maisy haven't seen Matthew and Beth for two years. Clare has no interest in urging the children to maintain the relationship.

The phone calls dwindled to a trickle as Matthew and Beth grew up and became involved in their own lives. The content of the calls became more estranged as well. One day Colin phoned Beth and called her 'Bubs', as he had done from the time she was born. Her answer was curt and to the point: 'Pa, I'm not a baby any more. Please call me Beth.'

There's a possibility Colin and Maisy won't see their grandchildren again. A large chunk of their hearts feels torn away. They pine for the children. The aluminium dinghy Colin bought to surprise Matthew for his tenth birthday rests against the jetty, unused. Colin won't sell it or use it. It just sits there.

Divorce. It's part of our times. It's part of our culture. The tragedy of its fallout some days seems endless.

The Brady Bunch Nightmare

'God grant me the serenity to accept the things I cannot change, the courage to change the things I can, and the wisdom to know the difference.'

If you've been lucky or smart enough to have created a happy 'Brady Bunch', you needn't read on. Otherwise, the one thing that's not going to change is the definite fact that, for most, step parenting is a no-win special. When it comes to relationships, the politics involved in step families make the back room at a Labor caucus meeting look like a play group conducted by Humphrey B. Bear. Here's why:

1. Blood is thicker than water. 2. New spouses want acceptance. 3. Usually, kids hate them. Relationships are hard work under the best of circumstances, so just throw these three little facts into the blender, and see how you go.

There is no love blinder than the love of a parent for their child. If a parent deems their offspring endangered, they will run into burning buildings, dive into huge seas, leap tall buildings at a single bound and always take sides with the child against the step parent. It's not insensitivity, or a lack of care for the partner, or even bias. It's nothing as cerebral as that. It's raw gut instinct. A lioness and her cubs. An eagle and his chicks.

When a person enters a new relationship where the partner has children, often, and especially if they have no children of their own, they make the mistake of thinking that this is going to mean that there are now even more people to love and be loved by. They know how important the children are to their partner and want to be accepted and approved of by them. Some even intuitively know the success of the relationship hinges on this very acceptance. So they try hard to please — very hard.

The potential disappointment is even greater if there are two sets of children and the partners make the mistake of going into the relationship with 'yours, mine and ours' expectations. This is the mistaken fantasy that now everyone is going to have all the pleasure and excitement of extra siblings and new built-in friends. Sibling rivalry is bad enough among blood relatives, let alone when there's fierce competition for favour and attention with the enemy's offspring.

Now let's talk about the cleverest part of this difficult triangle — the children. If the parent is single because their partner died, a lot can depend on how long the parent and offspring have had alone together. The child can develop feelings of possessiveness towards the parent, as though they have now become the surrogate partner. The step parent can be seen as an interloper, an intruder on their turf. This situation needs to be treated patiently and sensitively. It's important to make sure the child is taught that all relationships are different and separate. They need to know they are not being replaced, that the new partner fulfils a different need, and that you still hold their natural parent in high esteem.

If you're single because of divorce, you're likely to have a different problem. If the children see you as the cause of the marital break-up, it can make that problem worse. Long, long after a divorce, children can still fantasise that one day their mother and father will get back together again. It's just a natural fact. Even if a child reaches school age where, now, children living with original parents are statistically in the minority, children still cling to the model of a 'Little House on the Prairie' existence. We may be jaded and blasé about divorce. They aren't.

Now that the parent has taken a permanent partner, all hopes for a positive outcome for their dream of a family reunion, a reconciliation, are dashed. There will never be a 'three bears' reality. It will now, and forever, be 'two bears' and an outsider.

That is, unless the child can do something about it. The solution is patently obvious. Get rid of the outsider. The one and only way of achieving this objective is to manipulate the parent into disliking the partner. The best method to produce the desired result is to force the parent to take sides on their behalf. The step parent and the child are now locked into an adversarial relationship, a battle to the death.

The biggest problem here comes back to the 'love is blind' part. I keep trying to sell my observation that children are simply short people. As people are capable of manipulation, deceit, guile and power plays, so are children. Try telling that to the father of a clever little daddy's girl! Or most mothers of any child. 'My child wouldn't do that,' or, 'he/she's just a child and you're the grown-up. You should be able to handle it.' I've had both step mothers and step fathers report that while a conversation of the above nature was taking place, the offending child could be seen standing out of view of the natural parent, bold-facedly smirking at the berated step parent.

The prototype characterisation of step mother as 'evil' is often a misnomer. For one thing, she may have started out as a perfectly lovely, well-intentioned, rational person who got driven insane in the battle, dug her heels in, and decided to be 'the worthy foe'. She may have determined that in the relationship sweepstakes, in the struggle to the death with the offspring, she wasn't going to be the one to get the bullet.

This warfare is a mistake because, ultimately, if it doesn't make her look 'evil', it certainly can make her look nuts. This only ends up a win for the child opponent. She's a lot better off not taking the bait, and not taking the step child personally. She should navigate around provocation in her own space bubble of autonomy, leaving the worrisome behaviour for the father to cope with. If the child's hook doesn't get you in, eventually they'll stop trying.

Another possibility for trouble is if the step parent is insecure within themself. They may have excessive emotional demands and feelings of inadequacy and dependency that they're looking to fulfil in the relationship. This can make them jealous and resentful of their partner's time and energy expenditure on the children. They want and need it for themselves.

These people can make life so uncomfortable for their partners that they issue a 'them or me' edict. If the parent decides on the partner the children can really suffer. They've lost one natural parent, either by death or divorce, and therefore the dream of the ideal household. They've lost the hope of a step parent substitute and now they've lost their other natural parent. These insecure partners can look like tall children.

The place where step fathers usually come unstuck is in the matter of discipline. This is where the natural mother tends to be a softie and the step father is a stricter disciplinarian. It's funny how if the step father were the children's natural father, the mother wouldn't object to the strictness, but because he's not, she finds it unbearable. Children are wonderfully attuned to this discrepancy between the pair and can be diabolically clever at rubbing the step father's nose in his thwarted attempts to rule their roost.

Having set out what I see as the pitfalls of step parenting, it's a wonder to me that anyone with their head screwed on straight would even contemplate such a no-win arrangement. I don't mean to sound pessimistic, it's just that I see so many relationships destroyed by couples being unprepared or unrealistic about what they're getting themselves into. Better forewarned and forearmed.

The situation has to be addressed and discussed at length. Do not assume anything. You have to be open from the start about what your expectations are, and what you consider to be the priority for your loyalties. You need to work out how you are going to handle conflict and resolution, because believe me, there will be conflict that will need to be resolved. Better to handle it in theory before having to handle it in reality.

The number one, most important issue to understand is that this is an arrangement that has come about because of chemistry and love between you and your partner. It has nothing whatsoever to do with any chemistry or feelings between your partner and your children, and vice versa.

Establish strict rules of behaviour, but give everyone permission to dislike each other. Everyone has to feel entitled to have the feelings they have about each other. It really is unrealistic to expect that, just because you love the principal, the rest of the cast of characters are going to feel the same way towards each other as you do. The less you force this issue, the better the chance everyone will have to achieve at least an environment of mutual respect. And if you get that, be grateful and consider yourself lucky.

A laissez faire approach is the best one. Let everyone work out for themself their own individual relationships. If your partner is stricter (without being over the top) than you are, you really are stifling their self-expression when you thwart them. The children will work out how to navigate a path around them, the same way they do in two-biological-parent homes.

It's the natural parent's responsibility to endeavour to protect the step parent's image. Keep all discussions private. Maintain a united front. Once the children know they have a toehold in the door that can create division, you're in trouble. A smart technique my mother used if she thought my father had been too harsh was to have a private discussion with him, then they'd come out and she would announce that my father had changed his mind.

It's best to err in the direction of indifference towards step children than of trying too hard. If you put the responsibility for the relationship working on the children and make them come to you, they'll respect you more.

Don't forget, the name of the game, when it comes to being a child, is 'Hey, pay attention to me!' They want all the approval they can get. Be willing not to grasp for popularity, but be satisfied with respect. If you wait it out, it shows consideration for their feelings, while at the same time demonstrating that you won't be manipulated. If you're willing to do this, you're quite likely to end up with popularity *and* respect.

Time for CHANGE

Up to this point you've been flexing your new relationship talents. You've had a shot at 'training wheels' partnerships. Some will be gliding on into a happy, contented forever, feeling armed with enough skills to see the relationship through, whatever dilemma may come along.

Others may be having some niggling doubts. 'Perhaps I romanticised. Maybe I painted a picture that I hoped was there, but wasn't really there. Maybe we aren't heading in the same direction. What do I do now?' There isn't one of us in a long-term relationship who hasn't wondered at some point about whether or not we've made a mistake or settled for second best. This section is about giving the relationship its best shot, in the face of confusion, quandary and possible change.

Alas, no matter how well-intentioned or prepared we are to get a relationship right, sometimes it doesn't work out the way we had intended. It's important to recognise when a relationship has passed its use-by date. We need to know if we've picked a partner who isn't playing the same game we are, and, if they aren't prepared to, what our options are, and what constitutes appropriate behaviour. It's important to set limits and boundaries within your relationships, so that you get your needs met and maintain your self-respect. If your partner insists on stepping over those limits, you must be prepared to leave the relationship.

I can't stress enough the importance of using what some call 'mistakes' as pieces of invaluable wisdom. What's involved in enlightenment is sorting out what doesn't work for us. It narrows the funnel of choice for the next time. Now you know more about what you *don't* want, you'll waste less time and be clearer about what you *do* want.

Still, it's a lot more difficult to let go of our dreams than to enter into them.

Leopards Can Change Their Spots

Look, I know. It's an occupational hazard, but I still find it irritating. I'll be at a dinner party, just like ordinary people, and someone will turn and ask me, 'What it's like to bang your head against a brick wall for a living?'

Not only is human transformation possible, but it keeps me in business. Like people who deal with the outsides of heads, who rely on people asking clientele where they had their hair cut, mine is also a word-of-mouth game.

This is the way it works. A person or a couple are a well-established, 'duck for cover, here comes so and so' item. Suddenly you notice they're not so painful to be around any more. As a matter of fact, they appear to be quite good value. Invariably someone will ask, 'What have you done with yourself?' Transformed pains-in-the-bum are usually quite good about passing the word, and so it goes on.

So, how do you get leopards to change their spots? It reminds me of that old joke, 'How many therapists does it take to change a light bulb?' 'It only takes one but the light bulb has to really want to change.'

The first step along the path of transformation is having the *intention to change*. I really don't know what causes it. It comes from the same place waking up in the morning and deciding that you want to learn to speak Italian comes from. It's the germination of a seed. I used to be a non-Italian-speaking person, now I'd like to be an Italian-speaking person. I used to be a relationship failure, now I'd like to be a relationship success. I used to be shy, I'd like to be confident.

The second step is *finding a master*. The master can be a teacher, a course, a book, a video, a tutor or a therapist. You need someone who knows more about what you want to learn than you do. You may need a series of teachers. Every master has a ceiling on the limit of their knowledge. They may not be able to get you as far as you want to go. It's very important to be aware of this because most teachers are dedicated to their methodology.

Some think theirs is the only or the best technique. Although their method may work for many, it may not work for you, or it may not be enough. If you've taken a teacher to the limit of what they have to offer you, you're wasting time remaining their pupil. Take what you've learned and move on. Ultimately, you are your own master. There's a lot of wisdom in knowing what you need to know. Listen and follow your instincts.

The third step is a subtle one and can be overlooked, but it's the most important and requires the greatest respect. It's *readiness*. When people ask how long therapy takes, I always explain that it depends on the client's readiness to change. The *Chambers Twentieth Century Dictionary* defines the word 'transformation' to mean 'to change to another form'. What that means is moving from being one way to being another way.

Something has to be cashed in and left behind in order to make room for the new way of being. From ignorance to knowing, from safety to the unknown, from comfort to unease. It's saying good-bye to the devil that you know — and it's not always that easy to do.

Here's an example. Jane came to me and explained that she was in a destructive relationship. She wanted to get out of it, but was finding it hard to do. Could I help? 1. She had germinated the seed of intention to change. She wanted to go from being a person in a relationship that was bad for her, to a person who could get out of a destructive relationship. 2. She sought out a teacher to instruct her on achieving her goal. 3. My job was helping her to get ready.

Here's what happened. In the course of our discussions, it turned out that she'd had a close relationship with her father. At the age of nine he walked out on her and her mother, who was an alcoholic. Because of her mother's bitterness about her husband leaving, she hit the bottle even harder. Jane considered her to be quite inadequate as a mother figure. She felt she'd been abandoned by both parents.

What became obvious in therapy was that Jane was dealing with a larger topic than simply the personality of her boyfriend. She was dealing with the whole issue of separation and dependency and coping with life on her own. In the beginning, the very thought of being alone could make her feel ill.

There was a false start, where Jane plucked up courage and kicked him out. By the time his hand reached the door-knob, she was begging him to stay. When she came to her next appointment after that happened, she said she felt hopeless and ashamed. I pointed out that was unnecessary. All that happened was she did something before she was ready.

To enhance readiness, all you have to do is keep your eye on what your original intention is. You need to give yourself enormous permission *not* to be ready. Not being ready doesn't mean that you're a failure, or stupid, or lacking courage. It just means that you're not ready.

Watch a busload of children on a swimming pool outing. Some run up the ladder and jump off the high diving board before the bus engine is turned off. Others get in at the shallow end and submerge themselves a centimetre at a time. Some don't go in that day. Everyone's level of readiness is different, not better or worse, just different.

I instructed Jane to take the pressure off herself and go back into the relationship. For the time being, the security of having someone in her life, even if he wasn't good for her, served a higher purpose than getting her real needs met. She wasn't to push herself or berate herself. Every time she felt like sacking him and didn't, she was just to acknowledge she wasn't there yet: 'I'm in a relationship that's bad for me, but I'm not ready to get out of it yet.' She'd know in every pore of her body when the time was right. Jane's readiness took another month.

That was over a year ago. After she made him leave, she exulted in her independence. She flexed her 'I can make it on my own' muscles. Last week she booked in to have me meet her fiance, and to get a reality check on the situation. I'm pleased to report to the leopard-spot watchers that Jane is engaged to be married to 'Mr Mental Health'.

As for banging my head against a brick wall for a living; that's hardly what I'd call being the midwife at the birthing event of human transformation. Look, things could be worse. When it comes to dinner parties, just think what gynaecologists must go through.

Just remember, if you think you're ready for change, be assured that change is possible — although some people take longer than others to realise how necessary it may be.

No-Win Special

I often say relationships shouldn't be any more complicated than tennis. All you need to play a game of tennis is someone else who wants to play tennis. The trouble is there are people who will tell you they want to play tennis, when in fact what they really want to do is sit at the baseline and do nothing, or else smash shots past your head. That's not tennis. That game is called 'screw you'. Some people play relationships the same way.

When Francois was fifteen, he got into trouble with the police. He'd been a troublesome child and went to a special school for delinquent boys. The discipline was brutal but his complaints to his parents fell on deaf ears. Someone stole a car for a joy-ride, and, because of his reputation, Francois was wrongly accused. Reform school was recommended. His mother was afraid of how wild and undisciplined he was, so she went along with the recommendation. Francois ran away from France, went to London and never went home again. He's now thirty-five years old and he's never stopped punishing his mother. She's apologised her whole life but he treats her terribly.

He became a street kid and an artist. Karen met Francois while she was studying law in London. She saw him as an angry, misunderstood bird with clipped wings. She saw herself as a rescuer. They fell in love and he became a relationship tyrant. She was more burdened by study demands but bowed to his needs in every way. The only way to keep the peace was to make sure Francois was always happy. Because Karen loved him, she conceded. She always had a sense that if she didn't, he'd leave. She was right. He would have.

A series of events sounded the death knell for the relationship. By mutual consent they moved to Australia and had a daughter. Francois was besotted with her. Karen got a university position teaching law. Francois floundered. His excuse for failure was that Australians are philistines with no cultural heritage, therefore ignorant to his creative genius. He won a place at an art school back in Paris. Even though she was earning more money than he would be, Karen was willing to throw in her tenured position in order to support his career. She felt it was worth it for the sake of his ego.

A pet peeve in the relationship was that he always kept his studio locked and she wasn't allowed to have the key. This was where he kept his books, his music collection, the things of importance in his life. She could only listen to his music if he was there. He refused to allow her to tape his music onto cassettes. Control at all costs.

Francois was interested in things Eastern. He enrolled in a meditation course at an ashram. Towards the end of the week, he called Karen. He'd been thinking about things. They had the most intimate conversation they'd ever had. He told her he missed and loved her, things he had never said, and that he was going to turn over a new leaf and allow himself to trust her. As a symbol of this, he'd give her a key to his inner sanctum. She was ecstatic.

By the time he got home, he'd changed. He'd not only reverted but he was worse than he'd ever been and had tantrums over nothing. He took on a new macho pose and insisted on being waited upon. As for the key to the studio? In her dreams! In answer to 'what's wrong?' it would invariably be, 'Nothing, unless you keep up the nagging. Then there really will be something wrong.' He was quiet, moody, argumentative, black.

After being provoked all one Sunday, she made the mistake of saying that if he found her so repugnant why did he bother staying with her.

That was it. As if on cue, the alibi he'd been waiting for had been delivered at last. He was out of there. She begged, she cried, she implored. It was to no avail. He moved in with a mate. He told her all plans for the future were off.

That was five weeks ago. He still comes around to see their daughter. He's still aggressive. In answer to 'why?' he responds, 'You had the insensitivity to tell me to leave when I was already feeling down.'

She explained she hadn't meant it. She had been driven to it by frustration. He doesn't listen. He won't wear it.

The puzzle for Karen is that Francois makes excuses for being around a lot. Somehow even though he's done what he wants, he doesn't seem happy. He isn't content and seems as agitated as he was before. She detects ambivalence. In answer to her question, 'Do you still love me?' he doesn't deny that he does. He says, 'Love doesn't matter any more. The relationship doesn't work. It's over.'

Karen's pain and confusion are legitimate. Her questions about what happened and what to do are well founded. These circumstances aren't uncommon and are always shattering. The answer is grim.

The clue about what happened lies in the fact that, to all appearances, the relationship had never been closer. This, in itself, was the problem.

Francois is damaged goods. He has a deep and abiding mistrust of and anger at women. It started with his mother to whom he was a favourite. In his mind she deserted him at a tough time in his life. His hypothesis is that no matter how much a woman tells you she loves you, when the chips are down, she'll abandon you.

Francois lives a life-long temper tantrum. He has women in his life who dote on him. He knows deep down they love him but he pretends they don't. This keeps them perpetually striving. It keeps him in control. It justifies why he's entitled to mete out such harsh punishment.

His predicament was that everything was getting too good. When he was away in the quiet of the ashram, he probably got in touch with how much Karen meant to him. And daughters have a way of working themselves into their father's hearts without them even noticing. It all got much closer than he had ever planned. At the moment he realised the depth of his feelings, he started his emotional shutdown. Operation freeze-out.

Karen would have been totally defenceless against this. She quite reasonably heralded his new intimacy as a cause for celebration. Her expectation would have been a rosy, loving future. What a shock to experience just the opposite.

The only hope is that Francois has gone too far emotionally. There's a possibility he won't be able to turn off his feelings as easily as he would a tap. But maybe he will.

In any case, Karen's best shot is to beat him at his own game. It's time he was stopped. It's destructive and cruel to know someone loves you but they behave as though they don't. Karen needs to confront him, to ask if he ever intends to forgive her for the 'transgression' of being pushed so far that she said something in the heat of the moment she's sorry for.

It begins and ends there. If the answer is 'no', she's in a no-win situation. She needs to pack her psychological bags and move on. She needs to protect their daughter from his indulgence in dealing out emotional vandalism where and when he sees fit.

Karen is sad, but, more importantly, she feels relieved, less distressed and less anxious. She finally understands what has happened. Even better, she has embryonic feelings of anger. How dare he play with her feelings in that way!

The next morning there's a message from her.

'Francois would like an appointment. That's OK with me. But I hope you explain to him that I wouldn't consider having him back unless he grows up. Unless he can make a full commitment to me and our daughter, he's useless to both of us.'

Game, set and match, Karen!

Give a relationship your best shot but recognise when you're in a no-win special. Sometimes *both* partners need to change their attitudes and behaviour patterns.

Chequebook
Tyranny

When it comes to nastiness and generalisations, it seems to me that women resort to scheming, manipulation and bitchiness. Men's evil is almost always accounted for by the ill use of power.

This is what showed up on Wednesday: Sandra Jones, aged forty-five (fooled me. I figured fifty-five). Married eighteen years. At home there was husband Patrick, children Melanie, seventeen, Isabel, thirteen, and son David, ten.

Patrick is an executive with an international office equipment company. His base salary is $125,000 a year, before extras. They live in a large home in a nice suburb. The house is decorated with the furniture they had in their first marital flat. It doesn't matter. They never entertain.

From the beginning, Patrick convinced Sandra that she had no head for things financial. She shouldn't worry about that side of their affairs. She was to tend to home duties.

Sandra never goes to the supermarket. Patrick buys what he thinks his family needs to eat. He does this on a budget of $100 a week for a family of five. All expenditure — clothing, household or personal — needs to be explained, substantiated and justified. Patrick's verdict is final.

Four years ago, Sandra developed a debilitating viral illness and spent the next two years struggling to recover. Whatever energy she had, she preserved for the care of her children.

Sandra did a lot of reading during that time. Much of it was self-help material. Something she read had an impact. She mustered the strength to get out of her bedroom and get a job, for four hours, two days a week.

She and her children were given no pocket money. Patrick always said: 'If they want to squander money, they can earn it.' The last time the children asked for money, they were made to crawl across the living room floor begging for it. They never asked again.

Sandra's reading led her to a course held at her local community centre. It was about abused wives. She had never put herself in that category because Patrick had never been physically violent. Except once.

Melanie had bought a teen magazine because it contained an exercise program for thigh slimming. She had it open to the exercise page while she methodically practised the exercises. Patrick came down the stairs, saw the magazine and took it up to his room. Melanie went up to retrieve it. Patrick saw red. He grabbed her by the throat, dragged her across the room and banged her head against the wall. She suffered a bruised neck, a black eye and was dizzy for a week.

Sandra wept with shame for her impotence during the episode. Why hadn't she called the police?

What her course did was put her in touch with her feelings. For twenty-two years she had been a robot, numb. This had enabled her to stay conflict-free. Patrick did with her as he pleased. It didn't matter because she didn't feel anything. That included sex. Now the very thought of having him touch her was repugnant. So he kicked her out of the bedroom. She was relegated to the sunroom couch. His bedroom was above her. He'd ride his exercise bicycle late at night and turn up the volume of the television and roll it around on its wheels at all hours. This was her punishment for denying him his conjugal rights; 'I put a roof over your head and feed you don't I?'

Finally, matters came to a head. Sandra's car had been written off in an accident which wasn't her fault. Their insurance company paid for the damages. Patrick refused to give her the money. If she wanted another car she could pay for it herself.

Melanie works after school as a waitress and Sandra used to pick her up from work at 9.30 p.m. because she was concerned about her walking alone on the streets at that hour. After the accident, Patrick refused to lend Sandra his car, or to pick up Melanie himself: 'It's character-building for her to have to walk. It didn't do me any harm when I was a boy.' One evening when Melanie got home, she was hungry. There was no food in the house. Sandra had gone without dinner. Patrick was eating a takeaway in front of her, Isabel and David and berating them for mismanaging their money. Melanie went bananas at her father. She called him every name in the book, before fleeing up to her room.

Her actions must have somehow affected Patrick. He grabbed the shopping list they were forced to submit to his scrutiny each week and took off for Woolworths. When he returned, he made a point of putting the docket where it could be seen. $140! Included in his parcels of treasure, amid the toilet paper and Ajax, was a deodorant. Isabel had put it on the list as a joke, knowing those toiletries were her financial responsibility. Before Isabel went to bed, she said to Sandra, 'See, Dad does care about us. He's not all that bad.'

Sandra heard me talking on a radio program, jotted down my name, then saved up and came in. After our two-hour session, the only thing left to work on were a few lingering reassurances that no, she didn't cause his behaviour nor did she deserve it. We talked about the fact that, on some level, she felt sorry for her husband. I reassured her of the appropriateness of those feelings. Men like Patrick and other bullies are usually insecure and pitiable. Unless Patrick is willing to do something about himself, nothing she could do would change him.

I checked out whether she was ready to cash in her victim card. She was. I worked on teaching her negotiating techniques, assertiveness and limit setting, but after digesting all that, she said she couldn't be bothered working on the relationship. It was over. Her children would be delighted. They'd been after her to leave for years. That Isobel's affection could be bought for the cost of a deodorant made Sandra realise that if she didn't make a move, she would be creating another generation of second-class females, and she worried that David might start to follow his father's example.

I'll never meet Patrick because everyone knows only 'nut cases' go to see therapists.

I've had similar but less dramatic cases, where the male's chequebook domination is based more on a chauvinistic belief in the myth that women are hopeless at money management than an ill use of power. Playing out role reversals can be effective in such cases.

'Tom, what we're going to do is make believe all the money belongs to Nadia. What you have to do is ask her for whatever expenses you need.'

'That's easy. I don't spend money like her. I don't need much.'

'All right, just go through a typical week.'

Tom: 'I need $2 for the bridge toll.'

Nadia: 'I've done a feasibility study. Between petrol, wear and tear, garage fees and bridge tolls, it would be cheaper for you to go to work by public transport.'

Tom: 'What, are you crazy? I've been driving to work for fifteen years. I like the convenience.'

Nadia: 'Sometimes convenience is just plain impractical. I'll be selling my car and using yours from now on, thereby saving all that money we spend on maintaining a second car.'

Tom is stunned. 'All right. I need $5 for lunch.'

Nadia: 'No you don't. It would cost a fraction of that if you took your lunch to work. You can make your own sandwiches.'

Tom is getting angry. 'I need $30 for my weekly lunch with the boys at the club.'

Nadia: 'That's OK. I support you keeping up your friendships.'

Tom is grateful.

If necessary, the Nadia of the story can put limits on beer intake, sports ground admission, golf fees and other such outlays. It usually doesn't get that far. All a man has to do is gain first-hand experience of the insult, humiliation and indignity of being interrogated and forced to rationalise his own financial judgment. He gets the point.

So, what's a fair thing? In my opinion, for couples where one works at home, the sooner a monetary evaluation is made of the market value of home duties and mothering, the better. At least it would give a basic minimum worth to the work of the domestic partner. Couples can negotiate from there, considering the circumstances, number of children, CPI, and so on.

There should be basic household budget management courses available for the home carer who feels insecure about their accountancy abilities, whether they be male or female. Even if they work part-time, they are likely to have the time and their finger on the pulse of the running of the home, making them the logical partner to run the chequebook.

The irony for Sandra is that until she irons out a divorce settlement, she will have more discretionary income in her control by receiving single-mother benefits, than she ever had as the wife of a hundred-thousand-dollars-plus-a-year executive.

For Patrick, the price for being a control freak will be the surrender of half of his disclosed amassed assets and a certain amount of what he's secretly stashed away. Patrick's deeply ingrained sense of male chauvinism, lack of respect for women, need to assert power and control over money and its distribution make him a bad candidate for change.

The cost of his chequebook tyranny is his family: his wife, who on some bizarre level he loves and is dependent upon, his son and his daughters, who will take from his role model what they will never tolerate in a partner.

Money may not maketh the man, but how he handles it sure tells a lot about his make-up.

Sandra changed for the sake of her children as well as her own sake. At this time Patrick is not relationship material. He's not interested in change — just like the woman in the next story.

Winning
Versus Being
Right

The great scientists devise an experiment and construct a maze of tunnels. A mouse and a human being are put in a holding pen. A piece of cheese is placed at the end of the third tunnel and the mouse is released into the maze. The mouse goes down the first tunnel, and then the second, and finds nothing. It goes down the third tunnel and scores the cheese. The scientists put the mouse back in the holding pen.

The scientists move the cheese to the end of the first tunnel. They release the mouse. The mouse goes back down the third tunnel, and then the second, and finds nothing. It goes down the first tunnel and scores the cheese.

The scientists put the cheese at the end of the third tunnel and release the human. The human goes down the first tunnel, and then the second and finds nothing. He goes down the third tunnel and scores the cheese. He is then put back in the holding pen.

The scientists move the cheese to the end of the first tunnel. They release the human. He goes back down the third tunnel, and again down the third tunnel, and yet again down the third tunnel, scoring nothing — *because that's where the cheese is supposed to be!*

You see, the difference between a mouse and a human being is that human beings are interested in being right. A mouse is more interested in scoring the cheese.

I'd like a dollar for every time I've had to deal with a relationship where I've been unable to sell the wisdom of that parable.

The statistics on which gender more often ends a marriage lean towards the female. In my experience, they have been the ones who, often at greater material cost, finally call it quits, their mental well-being taking precedence.

Men haven't been in the majority for a number of reasons. They've been able to get away with eating their cakes and having them too. They usually aren't as well equipped to be on their own. They have been more unaware, and more unconscious of any marital problems. 'Problem, what problem? If there's a problem, she's the one who's got it.' If they have been aware of problems, many haven't left because of the fear of losing their relationships with their children, their assets and their lifestyles.

'The times they are a changin'.' Lately, the traffic has been running in the opposite direction. Maybe there really is an upturn in the economy. 'Compromise at any price,' 'Peace at all costs' is getting too expensive at the level of emotional well-being. Men are beginning to see satisfaction in their relationships as an equal opportunity experience.

Michael's moving out was a long-considered event. He's aware that what's at stake is his relationship with his children, his home and what he sees as his hard-earned money. He's wrestled his guilt with a Herculean effort. He's aware of the effect his move will have on his wife and children. In his mind he's between a rock and a hard place. He calls me in a last-ditch attempt to stave off what he sees as the inevitable conclusion — separation.

In they come. Michael's reasons are familiar. No sex. No affection. No warmth. No sense of being loved or appreciated. He feels taken for granted and used. He always feels in the doghouse. He never gets it right.

Mariana is understandably a mess. She is a combination of anguish, rage and shock. Her retort to his complaints is a torrent of abuse justifying why he isn't deserving of any of the above rewards and why he is deserving of the punishment. 'He never listens. He's selfish. He'd rather fall asleep in front of television instead of accepting social engagements. When we do go out, either he's too tired to be any fun or he embarrasses me because he drinks too much. He says he'll help around the house but he always does such a half-baked job I end up having to do it myself.'

Michael is perspiring. I admire him for dobbing himself in for what he would have known would be a very punishing session. When Mariana comes up for breath she ends her diatribe with, 'And Saturdays, when he could be with me, he'd rather be with his mates playing golf.' I'm careful not to make eye contact with Michael. If there were a voice-over mechanism in the room, it would be playing, 'Why wouldn't he?'

The difficulty in the beginning of therapy management is a 'looks' thing. Women go strategically wrong by picking up on the male's guilt vibes and going for that Achilles heel. They trust that if they can succeed at making him feel a right proper bastard, he'll come back to the fold. They are very happy to demonstrate with a vengeance the depth of pain and anger they're feeling.

What they fail to see is that this manoeuvre works. It makes the male feel terrible about himself and there is nothing he wants more than to escape from the way she makes him feel. He's already moved out. He can't get back to the peace and shelter of his new quarters quick enough. I have another client in a similar situation who moved out of his house and into a friend's garage and thought he'd found heaven.

I see Michael and Mariana separately. I explain that although monstrously unfair, it would be a good idea if she could hide her agony and rage so that he can drop his defences, which will enable him to start addressing issues.

Mariana: 'You mean I'm supposed to be a good sport about him walking out of my life!' Maybe she can't but it would be a good idea if she could fake it, because he's asking me if it's a legitimate request that he sacrifice his life's chance at happiness. His point is that there may be someone out there who may love him for himself, who may think he has some redeeming qualities. He's come to feel that his only value to Mariana is what he provides for her, what she can use him for.

In working with Mariana, two things happen. It turns out there are some points about the marriage that are valid issues of dissatisfaction for her as well, such as lack of intimacy and a lack of respect for Michael's inability to set limits. Now that she's armed with what she sees as legitimate complaints, she gets some of her power back. She feels more on top of the situation.

The other thing is that, as time goes on, Michael is becoming more immune to Mariana's manipulations. So she preys on his soft spot: the children.

She tells him what kind of monster they think he is, how they won't be able to forgive him and how he'll lose them forever. He asks me if it's true that children never get over a parent leaving. I'm obliged to be honest. It definitely causes bruising, but the truth is, if properly handled, children can come through a divorce without irredeemable scars. In households where major parental discontent appears irresolvable, divorce can actually come as a relief.

As her therapy continues, Mariana's self-esteem starts to improve. She's losing her victim look. Michael starts to feel less under threat being around her. She gets a new haircut, buys some stylish clothes. She begins to strut her stuff. Michael is starting to wonder if he's done the right thing by leaving.

I'm beginning to think we've got a winner here.

Michael comes in. 'I took Mariana out to dinner last night. I was thinking I'd touch on the topic of reconciliation. Before I did, she laid it on me. There's nothing wrong with her. I was the jerk who left. I'm the one with the commitment problem. When and if I grow up, she'll consider having me back. Let me tell you, I'm glad she feels better in herself, but if she thinks she's sexy, appealing or attractive to me she's got another thing coming.'

I see Mariana. I ask her if she's changed her mind. Does she still want Michael? She says she does but it's quite clear she's not in any immediate danger of allowing him to win at anything.

Mariana won't hear that her inability to be wrong, 'Why shouldn't I be critical?' and her perpetual judging of Michael, 'Such a bastard after what he's done,' could prove fatal.

Michael has assessed the situation as hopeless. No amount of trying was ever going to score him the cheese. He's closed the door and moved on.

You see, what the great scientists discovered was, there's a big difference between being right and winning. Mariana lost her marriage but got to stay 'right' about it. Dead right.

Mariana couldn't change and so she couldn't save her relationship.

If you do decide to move on from a relationship, be aware that it could be a transitional relationship that you enter into and identify it as such — for the sake of yourself and your new partner.

Rebound
Relationships

It's Doug calling from Brisbane. 'Oh God, Toby! You were right! Louise wants space to think about things and time to herself. She wants a six-month breather to reconsider things. I'm in agony. What do I do?'

What I know and what is now becoming clear to Doug is the awful reality. There's nothing to do. The future prospects of his relationship with Louise are grim.

Doug went down in my books as being one of the angriest clients I'd ever had. Doug had a sister who died after a long illness when he was a little boy. All available energy in his family went into the care of this terminally ill sibling. Her eventual death left an equally terminal pall of sadness in his family from which his mother never recovered. Neither did Doug. He felt ripped off, robbed of childhood attention, affection and time.

In life's not so funny way of being a self-fulfilling prophecy, Doug had never had a relationship that worked. He was too angry and he saw all relationships as a dress rehearsal for abandonment and sadness. He'd start to get angry about getting dumped as soon as the relationship began. At first the woman would get frustrated trying to prove the sincerity of her affections towards him. The more she'd try to get close, the more threatened he'd become and therefore the greater his need to create distance. His most readily at hand tool for maintaining safety was anger. In the end, he'd be classified as being too much like hard work. He'd frighten them off.

He would trot out these disastrous relationships through his therapy as proof that he was right that no-one would ever love him. He refused to consider himself as the source of his results. Doug was a challenge. The more I'd advocate his lovability, the more he'd go out and prove me wrong. He may have been the angriest client I'd ever had, but I was the stubbornest therapist he'd ever encountered. Secretly we both wanted me to win.

Doug's work took him to Brisbane so we continued to work over the phone. Doug had called to tell me the good news. Her name was Louise. She had been married for seven years and had a five-year-old daughter, Annie. She was finished with her husband. She just hasn't got around to telling him yet. Now that she had met Doug and realised that there were good and caring men out there, it made an already unhappy marriage unbearable. She was out. 'Toby, this woman loves me in a way I never thought possible. I've never been so happy in my whole life.'

Every hair on my head stood on end. 'Doug, just be careful. This woman is only just out of her marriage. She's been through a bad emotional time. She hasn't had time to sort her feelings out.'

All to no avail. 'Gee, Toby. I thought you'd be thrilled. I

thought this is what you wanted me to be able to do. Here I go trusting a woman, giving my heart away, willing to believe her love for me is genuine and all you can do is be a wet blanket!'

OK. Therapists can get pretty protective at times. 'Doug, enjoy it. Be in touch if you need to.'

He didn't need to for eighteen months. They moved in together. Doug was as besotted with Annie as with Louise. He was thrilled with their affection for him and his new-found sense of family and security. They were a ready-made repository for thirty-six years of Doug's stifled love and emotions.

Louise couldn't do enough for him. She wrote love poems and hid them in his briefcase, under his pillow, in the glovebox of his car, in trouser pockets. She learned to cook Italian food. She wished she could go to work with him so they'd never have to be separated. About a year into it, Louise started to get restless. From the zenith to Doug's phone call took another six months.

Louise had come from an abusive relationship. Her husband berated her. He criticised and put her down. She had been long-suffering and unhappy, wanting to get out of her marriage for a long time, but feeling trapped with a small child. She was young when she got married and felt insecure in the ways of the world. Her self-esteem was low and she lacked confidence.

When Doug showed up in her life, it was as though she'd won the lottery. He was a relationship geyser about to explode. A potential looking for a place to happen. Each of their needs were the other's solution. Doug needed a woman to whom he could devote himself. Louise needed the restoration of her confidence and her self-esteem. She needed to feel loved. A relationship made in heaven? Not exactly.

When Doug called, he bemoaned, 'I've been used!' But that's not really true. A transitional relationship is called 'transitional' because it's a relationship a person has on their way from one relationship to another. Usually what that looks like is this: someone has a relationship that doesn't work because something about it makes that person unhappy. Most commonly this something generates feelings of inadequacy. Those feelings can come from the way the partner treats them or from having been rejected by the partner. In any case, the relationship is over. The rejected partner has wounds that need healing.

Along comes someone willing and able to nurse those wounds. The hurt person will cling to the nurturing new partner. The function of the new partner is that of restorer. They restore the ailing partner back to mental health. The relationship the needy partner is having isn't with the nurturer, it's with themselves. When the job is finished, when the needy partner no longer needs what the provider is there to provide, there is no longer a need for the relationship.

The transition is from a bad relationship with someone else to a good relationship with themselves. Now they are ready to have a relationship with someone else. Often the nurturer is not the appropriate person as the candidate for the next relationship.

This explains why the people who get damaged most often by relationships are the 'rescuers', those who collect partners who have clipped wings. Once the partner can fly, that's frequently what they do.

What Doug got out of this relationship was invaluable. It broke his drought. He got hurt but could see that it wasn't the end of his world. He experienced feelings he saw were necessary in his life. On top of loving Louise he also liked her and Annie. They will remain good friends. Friendship is a far more realistic form for their relationship needs. He is grateful for their companionship in a strange city. Louise appreciates that he is a wonderful father figure for Annie.

The next time he goes relationship shopping, Doug knows that if a woman is newly out of a relationship, he should proceed with care. He needs to monitor her progress in transition. He must be sure that she has completed her journey from a bad relationship experience with someone else to a good relationship with herself. Only after she's completed that journey should he consider whether or not she's a good bet for a relationship with him.

Getting Help – Before, During and After

One in three marriages ends in divorce — and that statistic cuts across the economic, social and intellectual strata of society. It certainly indicates the degree of difficulty involved in getting it right. Self-doubt can appear before we get into relationships. It can creep up on the most unsuspecting, established partnerships, and if the worst happens and the wheels come off, there are certainly going to be feelings of failure.

At any stage of relationship wobbliness it is important not to let pride get in the way of seeking good counsel. Talk to friends as well as professionals. Learning about yourself can be daunting. It may mean learning to do things differently, but there's nothing shameful about saying, 'I'm confused. I'm upset. I'm scared.'

By being willing to admit a lack of perfection and the need for assistance, you may make enough difference to be able to salvage the situation. Even if you can't, the universe will shift to say, 'You mean you're not perfect? Welcome aboard!'

✺

'I Do' ... I Think

P remarital counselling is a hard thing to sell, especially to the participants. If you aren't thinking your partnership is indestructible at that point of your relationship, you probably never will. The silly thing is that because of this feeling there will never be a better psychological time to discuss anything that's on your mind. The motivation to make changes and please your partner will probably never be as high either. Love is at its peak; there isn't the acrimony of long-held grudges and unspoken resentments.

By the time you've announced your engagement, usually family and friends have had an opportunity to give the intended a look-over to see if they pass muster. Everyone will give you their two cents' worth if you ask for it. Everyone is an expert at everyone else's relationships. I say that with only a bit of tongue in cheek.

The people you invite to give an opinion will be coming from different positions. Some will want the best for you because they love you. Others may be jealous for a myriad of reasons. Listen to them all. Some of what people will say may be hard to listen to, some will be a delight. It's the hard-to-listen-to input that can be your best friend. This feedback will help you to take into consideration another way of looking at your intended, make you ask yourself if their consideration is a consideration for you. It can be a consolidating process.

He/she is too old, they're the wrong religion, undereducated, selfish, lives for football and so on. Every time you grapple with another opinion it helps to make you surer of what matters for you. In the end, that is the only thing that counts.

Having said that, the only problem with the opinions of family and friends is that they are biased. Whether they are for the positive or the negative, they have a vested interest even after you have considered what they have said, and been forced to vote on their feedback in terms of how it impacts on your decision, it is still a good idea to get some absolutely unbiased, neutral input.

Helena and Greg Adams were satisfied customers. Their marriage, which had gone seriously off track, was very much back on the rails. When their son, Brett, announced he was thinking of asking Lynda to marry him, their engagement present was a session with me.

Do I think that premarital counselling is of value? Here's what happened.

Lynda and Brett arrived at the allotted appointment a picture of young love. They sat with their hands entwined. They looked smugly uncomfortable. Brett said he thought this was silly, but since his parents had paid for it ...

I set out the rules of the session — this was an opportunity to place all cards on the table. Any shadow of a doubt, any question, no matter how trivial they thought it may be, was to be expressed. If they held back out of embarrassment they had no right to complain later.

I asked them to trust me. No matter how hurtful their communication to each other, by the time the session was over they would feel relieved, having got it off their chests. My offer was that we wouldn't stop until all issues were clear and resolved.

I explained that every couple I'd ever counselled confessed there was something they felt would iron itself out *after* they got married. I told them there were few relationships where one party didn't think they would be able to eventually *change their partner* into being what they needed them to be. The divorce statistics pay tribute to the fact that marriage is entered into by people filled with unrealistic expectations. Marriage based on reality has a far better chance for survival than marriage based on dreams.

No takers.

'Brett and Lynda, you're twenty-seven and twenty-four. How do you feel about monogamy?'

In unison, 'Fine.'

'OK. I have this printed form with a pretend marriage vow. It's routine. I always use it in premarital counselling. I've filled in the blanks with your names. Do you mind reading this out loud to each other?'

'No problem. I, Brett Adams, have totally thought out and completely understand that what I'm about to do is swear before Lynda, my wife to be, gathered family and friends, that I will never, never, never engage in sexual activity with another woman as long as I shall live. I include in this promise my complete awareness that throughout my life I will have acute and severe attacks of the "wannas". I'm going to want to have an affair with my secretary. I'm going to want to say "yes" to Michelle Pfeiffer when she says, "pleeeease". But I know that I can trust myself because my love for Lynda is so strong that it will allow me to resist temptation for ever and ever, so help me God.

'Holy mackerel!' Brett's complexion is beginning to blend in with my philodendron.

'What do you mean, "holy mackerel"? What's the problem?' Lynda looks perplexed.

'I just never thought about it like that. It's so final. Sometimes Lynda isn't in the mood for sex. What if that were to go on for a long time? What if I were really horny and Lynda didn't feel like it, and I went out for the night and had just a quick one-night stand. Nothing meaningful. That's only fair isn't it?'

Lynda has discarded Brett's hand as though she's discovered it has a socially transmittable disease. She's crying and is headed for the door.

Brett: 'What did I say that was so wrong? I'm just being honest. Lots of guys do that. It doesn't mean they don't love their wives. It's just that sometimes men feel like they don't get enough.'

Lynda looks at me imploringly.

'Brett, there's hardly a marriage where there isn't one partner with a stronger sexual urge than the other. The situation could be reversed. It could be Lynda who has a greater sexual appetite. It wouldn't be all right if she solved that with quick one-night stands either. Non-monogamy simply doesn't work. The issue here is that you are the one who's going to be the one compromising. You're the one who's going to be asked to make a sacrifice, to do without. Commitment calls for the willingness to go through periods of discomfort and stay faithful anyway. You may not be ready to be committed on that level. I think you should think about it.

'In the meantime, is there anything about Lynda you would change if you had a magic wand?'

Because Brett has landed himself in the doghouse, he's now more forthcoming.

'Well, actually, there is something that bothers me. Lynda has this ability to shut me out. It's like she's got this secret place she goes to, where no-one else can get in. When I ask her what's wrong, she says "nothing", but I can sense there is. When she's distant like that it makes me feel insecure and lonely. She turns away from me completely. I find that scary.'

Lynda looks sheepish. 'I do that when I'm angry at you. I didn't know it upset you so much. I should tell you what's bothering me instead. I won't do it any more. I'm sorry.'

Brett: 'Actually, it's not the sex I miss so much as the closeness.'

Brett and Lynda are back in hand-holding mode.

One in three marriages is statistically doomed. That leaves two-thirds who don't actually go ahead and officially obtain divorces. Some stay married because of religion, children, finances, appearances, fear or inertia. It may be the circles I travel in or an occupational hazard, but at least half of the two-thirds still married don't look all that happy. That leaves the final one-third of marriages where the participants live in a state of uncompromised happiness.

Of course, I didn't relate these numbers to Brett and Lynda. I totally support innocent, smug bliss. As long as it's reality-based.

Premarital counselling? You're mad if you don't.

Friends and Mates

If I took a free association test and they held up a card that said 'yummy', I'd answer, 'chocolate chip ice-cream'. If the card said 'holiday', I'd say, 'Cairns'. If it said 'friendship', I'd say, 'sanity'. One thing Cyndi Lauper got right is that 'girls just want to have fun'. And there's a particular kind of fun a girl only has with girlfriends. It's just different than the kind of fun she has with male friends.

Here's an example. I have a client, Angela, whose oldest friend is Bettina. They took leave of their spouses and went to Surfers Paradise together for a week. One evening, after they'd shopped till they'd dropped and feasted on seafood with a wonderful bottle of white wine, they went back to their hotel.

They started reminiscing about high school days. Angela asked Bettina if she was on the mailing list for Sonia Dwyer's annual Christmas newsletter. Sonia had been a member of their high school clique. Everyone in their group was there on merit. The merits were all different. Angela qualified because she was beautiful, and Sonia because she was very clever.

Sonia was scrawny, a later developer and therefore a 'late bloomer' with the boys. Then she hit the jackpot. She ended up with James Blake. James had money and prestige. Sonia was the first to have a nanny, her own Mercedes, and trips to travel page destinations.

If Sonia harboured any resentment about blooming later than the rest of her friends then it could have been the Christmas letter that she used to show it no longer mattered. Each member of the family, including the dog, got their own mention: 'It was a great honour to be promoted to senior partner in the firm . . . Merry Christmas, James,' 'I was very lonely when the two-legged Blakes left me for the month of January to ski in Aspen . . . bow wow, Spot.'

Getting back to their week away, Angela and Bettina decided to write an anti-Christmas letter. They made several drafts detailing failed careers and shattered dreams; earring-studded, Mohawked, drug-addicted children; bankrupt, chemically depressed third husbands; New Year's resolutions about Weight Watchers and poor Spot who had to be put down due to worms. They ended up tear-stained with laughter.

Angela's story reminds me of friends of mine. Pat goes back the furthest. It was our sense of humour that got us through our tortured teens. To this day, none of our stories need preambles, we know everything there is to know about each other. There's also Samantha who was there when a significant relationship ended. There's Laura who tells me to go back to my room and 'rethink my outfit', and who, on my annual sojourn back to New York, organises my culture calendar and fast-tracks me up to speed. Then there was Sharon, my next-door neighbour, who, upon learning that I was leaving for Australia, never spoke to me again. I thought my heart would break.

A lot has been said about Australian mateship and I think it's terrific. It's a war zone out there for men, these days. I think a bit of time around 'friendly fire' would be a welcome respite. Men's friendships look nothing like women's. Where men tend to gather at the local watering hole and discuss sport, politics and share prices, women lean towards lunch, shopping or the phone. The topic is often relationships, sex and things intimate.

My husband has a group of friends he's had for forty years. They meet every Monday for lunch and call themselves 'the cowboys'. They were 'buckaroos' when they started and are 'old cow hands' now. They've been through the Second World War, the rebuilding of their careers, their marriages, their kids, their divorces, their business successes and failures, and now they share health issues. When I ask him what they discuss he tells me it is about Australia becoming a republic, or how the North Sydney Bears played on the weekend, or who got the most burned in the Walker share float. I personally think lunch with 'the cowboys' would be a punishment.

After I've had dinner with my friend Julie each Wednesday night, he asks me what we discussed. I tell him we mostly talked about how our businesses are going, my son's relationship break-up, her daughter's pregnancy, our thoughts on liposuction and whether she thinks my red semi-permanent hair colour suits me. I can see him nodding off while I'm talking.

Neither of our events would have been the same had a member of the opposite sex been present. And both of us, as a couple, are better together as a result of our meetings outside the relationship. Because of the contribution made to each of us from an outside source, we're both more enriched and energised and have more to share with each other.

The function of friendship seems to be the same for both sexes. Friendship should be a pressure-free zone. It's where you can let your guard down and be your real self, with no need for gender role-playing. You can talk about what's really going on in your life with someone who will listen and not judge, who will listen and not advise unless you ask them to, who will simply listen and let you know that you've been received. By the end of the meeting, what you should feel is understood, experienced, nurtured and that there's been a shared interchange.

Friendship should act as life's personal clearing house. No matter how you go into it, you should come out better for having spent time there.

Curing a
Broken Heart

Ritchie Valens said it all when he wailed that 'Breakin' up is hard to do'.

To be perfectly honest, on a Richter scale, rejection has to rate an eleven. People often report that the pain is worse than a death. 'They're gone from my life, but they're still alive and out there. Unavailable to me forever.' The mind screams, 'Didn't they know it was *me*!'

The first rule about grief, agony and anger is: what we resist, persists, and what we experience, disappears.

What I'm saying is this: cry a lot, a lot. In order to do this you may have to take a broom to your social life. You know, those well-intentioned friends and family members who say things like, 'We all thought he/she was a creep anyway.' 'There are plenty of other fish in the sea,' 'It's been three weeks/months already. Don't you think you should be over it?' Or the classic 'My cousin Harold/Martha has fancied you for a long time, go out with him/her and you'll forget all about el creepo.'

Stick those people on a shelf in the wardrobe to be taken down later. You see, the predicament people have with your being upset is that it makes them feel impotent. They feel their job is to 'fix' it for you. The last thing you need is to have your problem *and* the problem your problem causes someone else!

What you want around you are people who don't need you to 'feel better', or not be in pain, or not be angry. What you need are people who understand that what's required is *listening*, not *fixing*. You want people who will give you permission to be the mess you need to be and not have that be a dilemma for them. So, grab the arm of a friend who's willing to take you to a restaurant while your tears spill loudly and freely into your soup. It should be someone who won't be fazed if the lady at the next table says to the waitress, 'I'll have anything *except* what he's/she's having!'

Emotional upset is a process with its own energy force. It has a beginning, a middle and an end. It's like watching a small child explode into a tantrum, with screaming, and pounding fists and legs, followed by crying and the odd yelp, followed by whimpering, followed by short jerky intakes of breath and exhales of sighs. If you asked the child to keep going, they couldn't. They're spent.

Think of yourself as a bottle into which has been poured a dollop of detergent, with the bottle then put under a running tap. It will erupt bubbles for a while, but eventually the water will run clear.

The second thing that helps enormously in a rejection is to remain focused on who your partner *actually* was. Resist your mind's tendency to want to dwell on the fantasy of who you thought/hoped they were or who you thought/hoped they would become. What you most often find in the reality of who they actually were is that they weren't truly committed to you. Maybe they never were. Because you wanted so badly for them and the relationship to work, you may have gone into denial about that; you didn't really want to know.

The degree to which you're willing to pull yourself out of the 'what ifs' and stay focused on the 'what actually was' will determine the length and degree of difficulty of your recovery. You'll start to lose respect for the reality of the person. You'll see their innate weakness that manifested itself in their not being capable of making a commitment. Nothing is a bigger wet blanket for passion than lack of respect.

The third rule about break-ups is *don't make any decisions* such as: 'I'll never love again,' or 'All men/women are bastards,' or 'No-one will ever love me the way I need to be loved.'

It's very important to differentiate between being devastated and not surviving. There's no easy fix for the first other than to ride it out, but when you are out the other end, notice that you can still wiggle your fingers and toes. You're still breathing. You actually survived.

Pick yourself up, brush yourself off and look right down the barrel of the gun called love, trust and vulnerability. Know that the price of relationships is giving that much of yourself away with no money-back guarantee. If it all goes hideously wrong it will feel as *bad* as it just did, but you *did survive*. It's the game of life. Your choice is to play it dead or alive. You can't win it if you're not in it.

A fractured heart should be treated as tenderly and sympathetically as any other fractured body part. Be very kind to yourself. It's appropriate to lead a 'bubble bath' existence for a while. Treat yourself to those expensive Italian shoes. Have that facial. Buy that bottle of Grange Hermitage. In time, you'll pour a glass for Alice/Ralph and propose a toast: 'Here's thanks for the fact that it wouldn't be Alice/Ralph's wonderful eyes I'm looking into now if I hadn't been bid adieu by that fickle one.'

Someone once told me about their friend Karl, who always grabs another woman if the one he's with leaves: 'I just wish I could teach Karl that being lonely is just another way of going through time.' So is being happy or bored or excited. So too is being broken-hearted.

Conclusion: stay inside your windows and away from lovers' leap. Not only does time heal all pain but it's been said that if you're lucky it also tends to wound all heels.

If you're in a long-term relationship that ends, it is important to get counselling to end the relationship properly.

Creative Divorce

When couples come to me for counselling, I confess. I let them know that I have a bias. I'm pro-marriage. If they've come to get help dismantling their relationship, I tell them they've come to the wrong therapist. That's not because I have a religious bent, or a 'make your bed and lie in it' approach.

It's that I've been there and done that. I've experienced my own and others' distress. I know that it's emotionally cataclysmic and that it takes a large bite out of a person's life. If it can be circumvented, it's worth going that extra distance to avoid it. I always say that you should only end a relationship if there's nothing left to do but end the relationship. That way, there's no looking over your shoulder wondering, 'What if I'd done this or tried that.' But, as I said, I'm no Mary Poppins. Some marriages are unworkable.

Obviously, it would have been better to have gone for advice before it reached this point, but if divorce is inevitable, it's important to get counselling. Here's why: when there's a relationship breakdown, it's because both parties have a relationship shortcoming; there is something defective about the way they both relate.

Even if one thinks the story is black and white, that there is a clear 'right' person and a 'wrong' person, for every Yin there is a Yang. There is a chemistry of opposites. That goes for both positive attraction as well as negative attraction. Statistics on the failure of second marriages bear me out.

The first aim of counselling is to make both people clear about what happened. The second purpose is to have a neutral person who can take a no-fault approach. And the ultimate goal is to be able to come out of your respective corners and shake hands. Trust me. It is worth every penny and every second spent in therapy to come out of a relationship failure with clarity, resolution and a sense of completion with your former partner.

In counselling where the therapy is a success but the relationship dies, here's what happens. The couple come in to discuss the reasons why the relationship doesn't work. Then, like peeling an onion, layer by layer, we get rid of the issues that each partner has. These issues would have excluded them from being suitable partners in any relationship. As each layer gets removed, the two take a new look at each other, to see if the change is enough to make it work. When there are no issues and no reasons left that are stopping either one from being capable of being in this relationship, and it still doesn't work, then it's over.

The advantage of breaking up a marriage this way is that both partners know they've exhausted every avenue, left no stone unturned and completely understand why it's happened.

It's called 'no-fault' divorce. I've have couples end therapy saying to each other, 'I really love you, but our relationship just doesn't work.'

They can feel confident their next relationship will be successful because of the skills they've learned in the therapeutic process. There are a number of reasons why a relationship doesn't work, but the most common cause of a marriage breakdown, when every other obstacle has been removed, is lack of sexual chemistry. If it can't work in bed, it's pretty hard to get it to work out of bed. Marital sex doesn't have to be the best sex, but it does have to be workable sex.

For couples who break up and get no counselling, here are some things to think about. Usually the decision to end the marriage is lopsided. Most often, one party wants it over more than the other. What this means is that one person is dealing with more pain and feelings of rejection than the other. Naturally, the person whose decision it is to end it would feel a lot less guilty if their partner would be happy, bounce back, cope and be friends. In a perfect world that would be ideal. Unfortunately, that's not the reality. The person in pain should have priority over the time span, and the design of any future relationship they may want with you.

If you want out because of another person, you may express the desire for everyone to be one big, happy family. This may work in Disney movies, but if you look at it, what you'll see is that this solution only serves *your* needs. You don't lose anyone, or have to feel bad about yourself, or have to feel guilty for the suffering ex-partner, but you're not really taking into consideration the needs of the person who feels dumped.

If you are the terminating partner, you have to settle for getting your need met by having the marriage over. You may not get a solution that's reasonable. In other words, the dismissed partner may find it too painful to be around you. Every time they are, they're reminded of what they've lost. It may be too confronting, too sharp. It may take time for the hurt to dull, or the anger to recede. This is simply the trade-off. You may not end up winning the 'most popular person of the year' award.

My advice for the rejected party is to grieve and get it out of your system. If you put it off, it will show up later. Get it over with. It's a mistake to run out and find a solution in the form of an ego tonic. Rebound relationships usually only last until you've used someone long enough to repair some splintered emotions. It's a plaster. When you take it off, the wound underneath will still need to heal. It's not fair to them and a waste of time for you. It's better to learn to be self-nurturing.

Try to stay realistic about the other person. Maybe they were never committed to you. And don't make any decisions about the future like, 'I'll never love/trust/marry/feel again.'

Often when there is a clear guilty party — a deserter, a basher, an alcoholic — a disservice gets done to the apparent 'victim'. Everyone will give the victim agreement that the other party was the guilty one and that the victim was hard done by. Unless the victim gets some insight into what their role was in the story, they are often doomed to repeat history in their next relationship. The victim has to stop needing to be involved with destructive people in order to get out of this dangerous cycle.

Although one party ends the relationship against the wishes of the other, sometimes that's because they were the first who was ready to say, 'It's not working.' In other words, often a relationship is dead and gone but no-one wants to be the one who tells the truth about it. Maybe the lingering partner knew it was over as well, but they preferred to stay in denial. If they admitted to what they knew subconsciously, they'd have to do something about it. Perhaps they weren't ready to accept the consequences, like letting go, hurting their partner or being alone.

The most important thing about a failed relationship is that you discover from it what it was about that relationship that didn't work for you. That way you can be very clear about what to eliminate the next time. Wisdom is not as much about knowing what you want, as it is about knowing what you don't want: 'It doesn't work for me to be with someone who needs to be saved' or, 'It doesn't work for me to be with someone who doesn't know how to be committed.'

What happens after divorce has to be reality-appropriate. In the worse scenarios, where there's been abusive, destructive behaviour, it may be healthier to sever all ties, close the book and get on with life.

Divorce needn't look like the *War Of The Roses*. Ideally, you got married for a reason. You probably weren't that stupid or lacking in taste when you chose each other. Perhaps you were immature or naive in your selection. Maybe you were in a certain phase of your life where that liaison had a purpose, served a need. Perhaps that form of relationship was wrong. Maybe, instead, it should have been a friendship. If that isn't what you have already, how about looking at turning it into that now?

Whether you decide you want to seek professional advice before, during or after a relationship, make sure you choose the kind of help that suits you.

Shrink Shopping

I t looked like the ink wasn't yet dry on her diploma, so when interviewing a psychologist to join the clinic at which I was working, I asked her how confident she felt. She answered, 'Very.' She had graduated with honours and won a university medal for an anxiety/stress reduction technique. I promised her that would come in handy. How do you interview a psychologist anyway?

Halfway through her first day on the job, I decided to see how she was going. I stood outside her door and heard sniffling coming from inside. I thought, 'How unfortunate, a tough case on her first day.' I waited. No-one came out. Time passed. The sniffling turned into crying. I knocked lightly. 'Come in.' It took a second to figure it out. There was no client in the room, only Natalie, the psychologist. She was the one crying. 'What happened?' I asked.

'Remember I told you about my university medal for anxiety reduction? Well, none of the clients were anxious. They were all depressed.'

It is my opinion that therapists are born, not made or

taught. They bring into the therapy room their approach to life. Like artists, they have an innate perspective, a way of seeing things.

Schooling teaches theory, tools and technique. Where good education is valuable is that it covers a broad range of what has already been tried. From this a student can weed out what they feel might work for them and what won't. This saves a lot of time in experimentation on one's own. Good courses also provide supervision, so you're not sent out to work with the public without some back-up support while you gain confidence.

What you learn are other people's theories and techniques. At the end of the day, every tool is just an aid. There is no substitute for natural endowment of perception and intuition.

Imagine a therapist to be like a CD player that could choose its CDs but if it didn't find one that suited, could play its own music. No matter how brilliant a student of human behaviour, in order to be instrumental in aiding human transformation, the therapist has to be greater than the sum of their CDs.

Here are some qualities to look for in a therapist: they need to be able to perceive your reality. Do you feel understood? Are they judgmental? Are they assessing you from their own reality? Do you feel accepted? Do you feel comfortable? The goals in therapy have to be your goals, not the superimposed goals of the therapist. Is the therapist able to focus? Are they talented enough to be moving you towards your goal?

Therapy involves a very intimate relationship. It is the therapist's responsibility to make sure that there are no confusing signals about the nature of that intimacy. If you are experiencing any sexual innuendo, it is important you discuss that with them. If you are not satisfied, leave them.

Be aware that everyone, in any field, has a ceiling on the level of their wisdom. If you've taken your therapist to their limit, the way you can tell is you'll start to feel frustrated and stuck at a particular point, unable to progress further. If that happens, it may be time to get some fresh input, another angle.

Keep in mind that therapy is a service industry. Imagine having a leaky tap and calling in a plumber. If she walked into your home and said she wasn't much good at taps but what she'd rather do is fix your downpipe, you'd sack her and hire another plumber.

All of the following can call themselves a therapist or counsellor. These are brief descriptions.

Analyst. This is the therapist you see in Woody Allen movies. In analysis, the patient lies on a couch facing the ceiling. If the patient's face were a target, the analyst is sitting at 1 o'clock — just out of view of the patient. Analysts utter few words, they take notes while the patient talks about whatever comes to mind, if anything. Their theory is based on catharsis. The thinking is that if you talk about an experience enough, you will get it out of your system.

In order to become an analyst, you need to have completed a four- to six-year course in one of three training centres, under the auspices of the Australian Psycho-Analytic Society, in Sydney, Melbourne or Adelaide. You need to have undergone your own analysis with another analyst recognised by the Society of Psychoanalysis. Analysis is the most expensive form of therapy. Traditionally, the patient goes four or five times a week for one hour. They are not licensed or covered by health funds unless they are a psychiatrist or a psychologist as well. If they are a psychiatrist, their fee is covered by medical benefits.

Psychiatrist. They interact more than analysts, the theory still being that the patient will talk themselves into good mental health. 'Active' psychiatrists are more interpersonal, use reflective listening where they reiterate back to you what you've said, and will undertake to have and share an opinion.

Psychiatrists complete a full six-year medical degree, then two years of residence in a hospital, then an additional five years of specialising at a hospital that treats mental disorders. They usually deal with the far end of the mental spectrum — the more seriously disturbed. They are very good at dispensing medicines and handling disorders that require medication. They can hospitalise and execute (no pun) shock therapy (although rarely these days). I have never worked without a psychiatrist as back-up for input, referrals and medication when necessary. Psychiatrists are licensed. Their fees are covered by Medicare, and if they charge the scheduled fee a visit will cost you nothing.

Psychologist. They complete a three-year university course followed by another honours year concentrating on the study of psychology, or else they do a four-year science degree. After they complete their formal training psychologists do two years work supervised by the Psychology Registration Board. Some go on to get a Master's degree which takes an additional two years and others do a Ph.D., which takes an additional three years. Those who do a Ph.D. are entitled to call themselves doctor because they have a doctorate degree in the philosophy of psychology. They are not medical doctors.

There are laboratory psychologists and clinical psychologists. The former set up test situations with animals to find insights into human behaviour. Clinical psychologists treat people they call 'clients' and problem-solve. Clinical psychologists are more interactive than analysts and psychiatrists. (I, personally, would do more talking in an hour than the client does.)

Psychologists have a licensing board. A percentage of fees for a psychologist are rebatable by M.B.F. Medibank Private and H.C.F. have no coverage at all. (Although they will assist you in buying gym shoes and getting hypnotised, they will not assist you in saving your family or sanity. Write to your fund if this makes you as angry as it makes us.)

Social Workers. They complete a four-year university degree. Upon graduation they qualify to become members of the Australian Association of Social Workers. They can do exactly what clinical psychologists do. They are not licensed or covered by health funds. (Write to your fund if this makes you as angry as it makes them.)

Psychotherapist. They may have done a course in therapy, but they don't have to. They are unlicensed and they can charge whatever they like.

Other people. Hairdressers, best friends, bar staff and grandparents. They have no professional training. They are simply the wise people of the tribe. They charge nothing and are often as spot-on as many so-called experts.

If you're seeking counselling, the best method is to go through word of mouth. The next best approach is through your family doctor. Failing that, you can always go through the yellow pages phone book. The questions you may want to ask are: is the therapist licensed, what are their qualifications, what are their fees, and briefly whether they think they are qualified to handle your particular problem. I've had clients ask me what percentage of successful relationship results I've had, and I think that's a fair enough question.

In the end it almost doesn't matter what the answers are, but it gives you a few minutes on the phone to ascertain whether or not you have a good feeling about them.

The mind is a very delicate entity. You may be in a vulnerable state when you go for counselling. Because of this, therapists are in a powerful position. Your instincts are important. Obey them and ask questions later. If it doesn't feel right, or you think you've exhausted this particular therapist's talents, get out.

When I first started practising psychology in Australia, I told a joke: in Australia, if you have a therapist, people think you're crazy. In America, if you don't, people think you're poor. Things are different these days. There isn't nearly the stigma. Hardly anyone gets through an entire lifetime where some neutral or third-party advice wouldn't come in handy. A good therapist at those times can make the difference between doing it the hard way or the easy way.

I've made my position clear. I think friends and families are indispensable. They are the salve that lubricates the gears that keep our lives running. They nurture the soul. They love and care about our well-being. It is because of this that they often miss the boat when it comes to being effective therapists. The reason is twofold. First, they are biased. They will advise us according to what they think will make us feel better. Second, there is often a tacit agreement between friends that the function of the relationship is to be 'agreement traders'. What this means is, I will tell you what or who is bothering me and you will agree that I am right and the other circumstance or person is wrong. And when you are in the same position, I will do the same for you.

Ideally, a trained, qualified therapist will not only care about you, but will feel for you as well. But, more importantly, they are trained to come at a problem with neutrality and detachment. They have no vested personal or emotional interest in the individuals in the story.

Often what is needed in sorting out a problem is a swift kick to a person's consciousness. A client may be there to tell you what a terrible person the other is. If I were an agreement trader I would tell the client they were right, that if only the other person changed things would turn out all right. That would disempower the client.

A therapist can give the client a way of taking responsibility for the part they play in the conflict situation. Although a client may not want to hear it, it will empower them to not only take action in this particular situation, but educate them to be enabled to get their needs met in any similar situation. Effective therapy should be more than a feel-good or agreement encounter. It should be an experience of liberation, mastery and empowerment. A person should walk away with a life skill that becomes part of the fabric of their inner self.

As a therapist, I have invited you into my rooms. I have introduced you to real clients. I have shared not only their problems with you, but also my solutions and interactions. Perhaps a situation has twigged a nerve and you've recognised yourself. If you've connected and taken on board any of the advice offered and feel you can implement that advice and effect change in your life as a result, you now have a first-hand experience of what professional therapy is. If you feel as though a personal journey has begun, I hope I have inspired you to take that pilgrimage through to its completion.

In the end, I pray that all of us, throughout life, will find good counsel and have the wisdom to recognise it, wherever it appears.

Tobyisms

1. The three essential ingredients of a relationship: Love, chemistry and commitment. Love is the least important aspect and commitment is the most important — as long as there's chemistry.

2. We're capable of loving anyone. The man I'm committed to is the person I'm doing something about it with.

3. What commitment *is*: When you feel like bopping your partner over the head with a frying pan, it's not love, lust or passion that gets you home, it's commitment.

4. What commitment *isn't*: 'Do you really love me?' 'Well, I'm here aren't I?' That doesn't mean anything. Everyone has to be somewhere. If you don't know whether you're committed or not, you're not.

5. 'The one': There's no such thing as 'the one'. When you're ready for a relationship, the person sitting next to you on the bus could be the one.

6. *Real*isation: The ability to make your partner feel they are real to you, rather than an object or the projection of someone from an earlier relationship.

7. A man's favourite thing is to be adored. A woman's is to be understood.

8. If I ask you to hug me, please don't …. me.

9. 'No decision' at some point becomes a decision in itself. The person waiting needs to act accordingly.

10. Taking things personally: When you take others' behaviour and form a 'to me' bridge.

11. Resentment: You do something I hate. I don't tell you clearly what that something is. And every time you do it, I put one more nail in your coffin.

12. A 'no-win special': You're damned if you do, and damned if you don't.

13. Jealousy: When you see someone walking down the street with a sour expression on their face. Their best friend probably just won the lottery.

14. Guilt: Nice person's disease. I do something really rotten, then I feel terrible about it. That lets me know that I'm a nice person, because only awful people do bad things and don't feel guilty.

15. Unconscious: A person who knocks a coffee cup off the table is unaware. A person to whom it never occurred there would be a coffee cup on the table or, having knocked it over, they're meant to do something about it, is unconscious.

16. Rejection: To think rejection is an impossibility is to be a fool. To live life as though it's a probability, is to be a coward. You've got to be in it to win it.

17. On breaking up: Pick yourself up, brush yourself off and look right down the barrel of the gun called love, trust and vulnerability.

18. A 'survival decision': When I grow up I'm never going to let this happen to me again — out of my control. But in order to have a good relationship, you will have to be prepared to question this decision and to take a risk.

19. The price of a real relationship is the risk of total devastation. Only those who know they will survive are capable.

20. The voice of truth for you: This is the gut or heart voice. It says what you really want, what is really true for you.

21. The three 'gets': Get real. Get over it. Get a life.

22. 'Having a fabulous life is the best revenge.' (Levis ad.)

Suggested Reading

Biddulph, Steve. *Manhood*, Finch Publishers, Australia, 1996.

Comfort, Alex. *The Joy of Sex*, Gary Allen, Australia, 1991.

Dowrick, Stephanie. *Intimacy and Solitude*, Heinemann, Melbourne, 1991.

Gray, John. *Men are from Mars, Women are from Venus. A practical guide for improving communication and getting what you want in your relationships*, Thorsons, London, 1993.

Jampolsky, Gerald. *Love is Letting Go of Fear*, E.J. Dwyer, Australia, 1979.

Kopp, Sheldon. *If You Meet the Buddha on the Road — Kill Him*, Sheldon Press, Great Britain, 1994.

Norwood, Robin. *Women Who Love Too Much. When you keep wishing and hoping he'll change*, Simon & Schuster Pocket Books, USA, 1985.

Peck, M. Scott. *The Road Less Travelled*, Random House (Rider), USA, 1993.

Williamson, Marian. *Return to Love*, HarperCollins, Australia, 1992.

Index

affection, 125, 128

analysts, 229–30

blended families, 166–72

broken marriages, 221–26

budget *see* money

change, 173–74, 175–79
  inability to, 193–98
  intention to, 176
  means of, 176
  readiness for, 176–78
chemistry, sexual, 31–34, 223, 235
children's choice of partner, 137–41
choices, owning, 18–22, 95
clinical psychologists, 231
Comfort, Alex
  The Joy of Sex, 126, 237
commitment, xii, 35–36, 37–39, 211, 235
  lack of, 62, 64, 67, 219
communication, 49, 53
compliments, 133
control, 24, 28, 80–81, 86, 236
counselling, 205–06
  divorce, 221–26
  premarital, 207–12
counsellor, choosing a, 227–34

decisions, 235

denial, 62–65

dependency, 90

divorce affected grandparents, 162–65

divorce counselling, 221–26

domination, 19–20

emotional upset, 218

empowerment, 233

excuses, 84

extracurricular sex, 108–11

failed relationships, 222–26

family relationships, 135–72

fathers
  'my little mate' syndrome, 146–48
finance *see* money

flirting, 133

friendships, 125–26
  becoming sexual, 103–07
  and mateship, 42, 213–16

gets, the three, 236

good news, bad news technique, 16–17

good relationships, 31–36

grandparents, divorce affected, 162–65

guilt, 14, 236

guilt deflection, 13–17

guilty parties, 224

help *see* counselling

impotency, 25
incompatibility, parent/child,
    156–61
infidelity, 112–118, 119–24
    men's, 112–16
    women's, 116–17
intimacy, 57–61, 126, 128–29

jealousy, 71–77, 236
Joy of Sex, The (Comfort), 126,
    237

knowing oneself, 1–2, 3–8

laboratory psychologists,
    231
love, 27, 34–35, 235
love addiction, 89–95
love deprivation, 89–90

marriage breakdown, 221–26
mateship and friendship, 42,
    213–16
men
    differences to women,
        109–11, 235
    identity, 6–7
    sexuality, 119–22
    understanding, 40–45, 46–51,
        235

women's communication with,
    50, 96–100
money
    as cause of conflict, 10
    as tool of power, 186–92
mothers, professional, 143–46

needs of women, 44–45, 53–65
negotiation, 53–56
no-win special, 18, 20, 180–85,
    236

obsessive jealousy disorder,
    74–75
'one, the,' 235
only child-itis, 91–92
other woman, the, 44, 66–70

pain management, 80
parental relationships, 23–28
parent/offspring relationships,
    137–41, 142–48, 156–61
partners of love addicts,
    92–93
perfectionism, 9–12
personal best, 12
powerlessness, 25
premarital counselling, 207–12
professional mothers, 143–46
psychiatrists, 230
psychologists, 230–31
psychotherapists, 231

readiness
  to change, 176–78
  to stop denial, 65
realisation, 235
real me, the, 5
rebound relationships, 199–203, 224
reflective listening, 133
rejection, 83, 217–20, 236
  causes, 86
  recovery from, 218–19
relationship, xi–xiii, 1–2, 29, 31–36, 235, 236
repetition in relationships, 78–83
requests, 54–55
resentment, 15, 127, 235

seduction, 133
self-acceptance, 12
self-esteem, 94–95
sensuality, 101, 125–30
sexual chemistry, 31–34, 105, 223, 235
sexuality, 101, 119–24, 126–28
'should' voice, 5–8
social workers, 231
standing up inside yourself, 94–5
Steinem, Gloria, 40, 42
step families, 166–72

superego, 14
survival decisions, 80, 236
survival issues, 29–30, 79–80

teenagers, 149–55
therapist, choosing a, 227–34
therapy, 94–95
thoughts and feelings, 6–8
transitional relationships, 202–03, 224
truth for you, 236
'truth' voice, 5–8, 236
tyrants, 90–91, 93, 181

unconsciousness, 236
users and used, 14–17

violence, 75, 187

win-win relationships, 49–51
women
  communication with men, 50, 96–100
  differences to men, 109–11, 235
  identity, 7
  sexuality, 120–21, 122–23, 127–28
  understanding, 131–34, 235
  see also other woman, the
women's movement, 40–44